THE
A love story that changed
ROYAL
the power dynamics
SCANDAL
in British India

RRASHIMA SWAARUP VERMA

An imprint of
Srishti Publishers & Distributors

Srishti Publishers & Distributors
A unit of AJR Publishing LLP
212A, Peacock Lane
Shahpur Jat, New Delhi – 110 049

editorial@srishtipublishers.com

First published by Bold,
an imprint of Srishti Publishers & Distributors in 2022

10 9 8 7 6 5 4 3 2 1

This is a work of non-fiction, based on the author's thorough research of Indian history. Some events have been fictionalised for dramatic effect. While due care has been taken to verify all information at press time, any inadvertent miss brought to notice shall be updated in the subsequent editions.

Printed and bound in India

Praise for the book

"...marvellous work set against the backdrop of the British relationship with the Nizam of Hyderabad. It is a brilliant narration of how politics impacts the love story of a British Resident and a Hyderabadi noblewoman. It is a meticulously researched narrative with a simple style that can be easily followed by the reader."

– Dr. Aruna Pariti.

Head – Department of History
Osmania University, Hyderabad

"This is history writing with its moistness retained. Thoroughly researched and extremely readable."

– Dr. Shankar Kumar

Department of History
Hindu College, Delhi University

"An epic tale of love and war. Rrashima's style of writing is simple and fluent to keep the reader involved and expresses her great knowledge of the subject."

– Salma Yusuf Husain

Noted Persian Scholar, Author and Food Historian

"Brilliant and evocative, transports you to the unhurried era of the Nizams' benevolent time."

– Diwan Gautam Anand

Noted Columnist, Famed Hotelier and Sufi Poet

"Rrashima weaves pulsating, intriguing, luminous strands of emotions around love and war, deceit and faith, in this historical romance that moves the heart with its consequences."

– Ashwini Bhatnagar

Noted Journalist, Author and Documentary Filmmaker

"The author's style is appealingly a blend of the descriptive and narrative. Each character comes alive through the tiny differing nuances designated to them. Overall – a definitely "want to read" book."

– Amita Sarwal

Freelance Lifestyle, Travel and
Architectural Journalist and Editor

"Rrashima creates a medley of tense, hair-raising moments in a war-torn land, and warm and fuzzy ones that are certain to leave the readers beady eyed. A taut storyline and well etched out characters are the USPs of this book, but what works for me the most is the extensive research that has gone behind painting a vivid picture of an era gone by."

– Anurag Anand

Bestselling Author, Artist and Corporate Professional

To all my fabulous readers.
Your love is the most precious gift for me.
After all, I write because you read!

A note from the author

Writing this book has been a truly rewarding and enriching experience for me. I have thoroughly enjoyed every moment and am immensely grateful to all those people who have contributed to this incredible journey with their kindness, wisdom and generosity.

First and foremost, I want to thank my brilliant literary agent, Suhail Mathur of The Book Bakers literary agency for his unparalleled support, faith, wisdom, and guidance. Suhail truly is agent extraordinaire. He has played a tremendous role in the journey of this book and has been there for me every step of the way. I am truly indebted to him for being such a wonderful literary agent, mentor and friend to me. Thank you Suhail, for everything that you do.

I want to express my heartfelt gratitude and appreciation to my wonderful publishers, Mr. J.K. Bose and Arup Bose of Srishti Publishers. Thank you for welcoming me into the Srishti family with so much warmth and for giving me the opportunity to present this beautiful story to the world. I feel truly honoured to work with you and your team.

Heartfelt thank you goes out to my lovely editor, Stuti Sharma Gupta for her extremely valuable input and guidance. I have learnt enormously from her and it has been a tremendous pleasure to work with a committed and brilliant editor like her.

While I was doing the research for this book, there were many wonderful historians, experts and scholars who whole-heartedly supported and helped me. I am very thankful to them for sharing their immense knowledge and expertise with me. I want to especially express my gratitude to Dr. Shankar Kumar (Department of History,

Hindu College, Delhi University), Dr. Aruna Pariti (HOD, History Department, Osmania Women's University, Hyderabad), Salma Hussain (Persian scholar and food historian), Ashwini Bhatnagar (noted journalist, author and documentary film maker), Anurag Anand (bestselling author and artist), Amita Sarwal (freelance lifestyle travel journalist and editor) and my dear friend Diwan Gautam Anand (famed writer, columnist, Sufi poet and hotelier) for sharing their very valuable input with me about the book. Their knowledgeable insights, encouragement and kind words of appreciation were a validation that I had done justice to this beautiful story.

My gratitude also goes out to all the channel partners who worked with commitment to bring this book to my readers. Thank you for being such incredible gateways to a beautiful world of books.

I want to thank my family for all the love and for being an unconditional rock of support, always. My mother Shirley, my father Swapn, my husband Puneet, and my darling son Eshan, who is a constant source of joy and inspiration in my life.

And most importantly, I need to thank you, my reader, for believing in me and making all the hard work worth it. Your support is precious beyond measure and I hope you enjoy reading The Royal Scandal as much as I have enjoyed writing it. Do see the QR code at the end of the book which will help you to access the will of Lt. Col. James Achilles Kirkpatrick, sourced from the National Archives, UK. It is an important historical document and will be interesting to view. Persian names have been hyphenated throughout the narrative as a stylistic regulation. You will also find a detailed glossary at the end of the book for your reference.

Once again, my heartfelt gratitude for your love and encouragement. That truly is the most precious gift for an author!

1
The British Residency

Hyderabad, 1798

'*Sahib*? More *chai*?'

The server was young, eager to please. Sahib usually had two cups after lunch and a cup after dinner. The spiced black tea was a good digestive and comforting too, particularly in these colder months. Today, however, James was not in the mood for a second cup. Shaking his head, he declined the offer and the server retreated, disappointed. The restive state of mind of Lieutenant Colonel James Achilles Kirkpatrick, as against his usually easy-going demeanour, hadn't gone unnoticed by the ample staff at the British Residency.

'He is in a strange mood,' whispered the server to one of the cleaning women as he carried the tray back to the kitchen. 'Absent-minded and sort of...distracted.'

The woman giggled. 'All I can say is that his absent-mindedness seems to have passed on to everyone at the Residency. Do you know that the *khansama*[1] actually over-cooked the lamb this afternoon? He has never done that in the forty years that he has worked as a cook.'

1 Khansama is a Persian word. Its lexical meaning - a cook who can also play the role of a house steward.

'Well, Sahib ate it without a word of complaint. This time, he did not even talk about the absence of potatoes.'

'Nor did he notice the lack of salt in the Mulligatawny soup[2].' The cleaning woman stroked her chin thoughtfully then. 'He really is pre-occupied.'

'Perhaps it was the card game yesterday,' concluded the server. 'I heard that Sahib lost every round.'

That was true. The previous night's card game hadn't gone well for James, which was rare. He was generally a skilful player, deft and sharp. It was a little hard to believe, though, that a mere card game could put a dampener on his usually cheerful spirits. With his agreeable disposition and easy laughter, James had, in the short time that he'd spent in the city, already become hugely popular among the noblemen, ministers, military men, bankers and even the courtesans that constituted Hyderabadi society. A regular attendee at most events, he enjoyed socializing of any kind. Weddings, *mushairas*[3], hunting expeditions, dance performances, *mehfils,* card games – he enjoyed them all to his heart's content. Last night, the card game had been at the mansion of Aristu Jah, the Prime Minister at the Nizam's *durbar.*

'That is another one you have lost. Your luck seems to be running out,' Aristu Jah had said with a laugh. A tall, full-bodied man, he was known for his wisdom and love for the arts. He was

2 Mulligatawny is a soup which originated from South Indian cuisine. The name originates from the Tamil words *miḷagu,* and *taṇṇi*; literally, "pepper-water". It is related to the dish rasam.

3 Mushaira is a poetic symposium. It is an event where poets gather to perform their works. A mushaira is part of the culture of north India, Pakistan and the Deccan, particularly among the Hyderabadi Muslims, and it is regarded as a forum for free self-expression.

certainly a clever politician and James sometimes lovingly called him "Solomon", after the wise monarch of Israel. And why not! After all, Aristu Jah had a uniquely sharp mind. Born Mu'in-ud-Daulah, Mushirul-Mulk, Azamul-Umara, he had been bestowed with the title "Aristu Jah" as a gesture of appreciation for his astuteness and loyalty. The area of Musheerabad was named after him and was a part of the substantial *jagir* presented to him by the Nizam. Of course, the one thing about him that had made a lasting impression on many was the way he had handled the Marathas after the Battle of Kharda in 1795. He had been taken as a hostage after the battle, but not only had he skilfully negotiated his own release, he had also managed the return of ceded territories to the Nizam, including the Daulatabad Fort.[4] He had been given a hero's welcome when he returned to Hyderabad and was reinstated in the ministry. There was certainly something remarkable about Aristu Jah.

'Well, have you not heard that famous saying?' James had responded to him then. 'Miss, you will have a sad husband, you have such good luck at cards. Perhaps the reverse is true as well. Unlucky in cards, lucky in love.'

'Ah, love!' Aristu Jah had stroked his neat beard and slipped his pipe back into his mouth. 'You be careful of love, my friend. It is wispy, elusive, like the wind.'

'The Syrah[5] certainly seems to have put you in a poetic mood.' James had smiled at the Prime Minister. 'That is your fourth glass already.'

4 Nanisetti, Serish. There lies a forgotten story. *The Hindu*. 19 August 2017.

5 Syrah, also known as Shiraz, is a dark-skinned grape variety grown throughout the world and used primarily to produce red wine.

'Like the fifth century historian Herodotus said, Persians are very fond of wine.' Aristu leaned back in his chair. 'So much so, that they routinely make important decisions after drinking it. Of course, they do reconsider those decisions the next day. Thankfully, we are not taking any major decisions today.'

Everyone at the table had laughed heartily. It was late and they'd all had a few glasses of Syrah by then.

As a matter of fact, the server's assumption that the card game had been the reason for James's distracted state of mind was not quite correct. Despite losing, James had been in high spirits throughout the evening, just like he'd been for several weeks now. But then, the general mood in the Company had been jubilant and celebratory recently. After many months of careful planning, intense negotiations back and forth and anxious anticipation, the British had finally signed the Subsidiary Treaty with the Nizam. According to the treaty, the Nizam would dismiss his French troops and maintain a subsidiary force of six battalions. In return, the British would guarantee his state against enemy aggression, including the Marathas.[6]

This was, in fact, the first Subsidiary Treaty to be signed by the British in India and a major feat for the Company. After all, the French had recently been a source of constant worry for the British. Then when the French General, Monsieur Raymond, passed away on 25 March, it presented the perfect opportunity for the British to seize control. The treaty was signed and the French troops disbanded on 21 October 1798. What a magnificent sight it had been! Now

6 Fuhr, Enid M. Thesis on Strategy and Diplomacy in British India Under Marquis Wellesley. King's College, University of London, 1988.

with this victory, Governor General Wellesley was exultant and that meant good things for James and his career in India. Of course, James's role in helping to diminish French influence in Hyderabad could not be overstated.[7] Following the treaty, Wellesley had already formally appointed James as Resident of Hyderabad, instead of just Acting Resident. James had been in a blissful mood since.

Today, however, he'd been feeling restless since the morning. They were now well into December, the weather in Hyderabad had been considerably cooler for days, and after lunch, James had spent an hour strolling in the flower garden outside. Strangely, even the scented flowers and melodious birdsong that he usually loved, hadn't been able to quieten his mind today.

He'd first heard about her from the female relative of a colleague. Admittedly, his curiosity had been instantly roused at the ardent praises. "Extraordinarily beautiful", was how she had described her. She'd then gone on and on, waxing eloquent about the young girl's creamy, flawless complexion, her eyes that were so like the stars that shone in the night sky, even the tiny beauty mark above her chin. 'She looks reticent, bashful, yet seems to have a quiet resilience about her,' the lady had finally concluded. 'There really is something utterly remarkable about that young woman.' It was hardly surprising then, that James had been intrigued from that moment on. Obviously though, despite visiting her home several times before, James had never really seen her. The women of that household stayed in the *zenana*[8] quarters, and always maintained *purdah*. Today, however, was the wedding of the older granddaughter and hundreds of people

7 Interview with Dr Shankar Kumar, Noted Historian, Hindu College, Delhi University. Dec, 2021.

8 The part of the house for the seclusion of women (in India and Iran).

had been invited. James was well aware that even weddings in Hyderabadi society were segregated affairs, with no intermingling between the men and the women, who always remained on their separate sides.[9] Still, he couldn't help hoping, wondering, whether today might be the day when he may possibly be able to catch a glimpse, see the face, perhaps even look into the dark eyes that he hadn't been able to drive out of his mind ever since the first time he'd heard about them.

Trying to push the restiveness away, James strode over to the ornately carved wardrobe at the end of his bedroom, the largest room in the bungalow. The bungalow, a part of the Residency building, was for the personal use of the Resident. It was a charming house on the Northern banks of the Musi river, but it had been made in a hurry, and was already in dire need of renovation. Now, as he flung the double doors of his closet open, James couldn't help recalling the remark of a friend who'd been visiting from Calcutta last month. 'This closet does not look like it belongs to an English officer,' he'd commented. James had smiled at the remark, but it was true. After all, he really was far more at home in the bejewelled *jamas, angrakhas* and *neemas* that occupied one side of the closet,[10] than in the full-skirted coats, breeches, waist coats and linen shirts on the other side.[11] He was well aware of the fact that his clothes as well as the *hookah* and betelnut, had invited many a raised eyebrow among

---

9 Interview with Salma Yusuf Hussain, Noted food historian and Persian scholar. May, 2022.

10 Deccani Style and Men's Fashion: Splendour Revisited. Salar Jung Museum, Hyderabad. Google Arts and Culture.

11 Interview with and research paper by Dr Aruna Pariti on "British Residency", Department of History, Osmania Women's College (Former British Residency), Hyderabad, India. February, 2022.

his own countrymen, since that sort of thing wasn't encouraged anymore. James, however, wouldn't allow the bigoted contempt of some prejudiced individuals to mar his affection for Hyderabad and India. That affection, that love, wasn't something he could change, because it was, now an intrinsic part of who he was.

Turning his attention to the left side of the wardrobe, James deftly twisted the key in the cast iron safe where he kept his watches, accessories and other valuables. Pulling open the door, he took out a long necklace encrusted with pearls and rubies as well as a gold pocket watch with cathedral hands. His valet had already laid out his clothes for the evening – a brocade jama in a deep shade of purple, a silk *kurta,* gold *churidar* and embroidered *khussas* with their curled-up toes. The outfit was elaborate enough to wear to the wedding tonight and as always, his valet had chosen well. James, however, preferred to pick out his jewellery and pocket watch himself.

Now he placed the necklace and watch on the four-poster bed and then picked up the jama and held it up against his tall frame. The deep purple looked splendid in contrast to his fair complexion, blue eyes and light hair, though of course, James was an extraordinarily handsome man. After all, he had inherited the striking good looks of his father, Colonel James Kirkpatrick. Born in Charleston, South Carolina in 1729, the Colonel had had a successful career with the Company. His first son, William, had been born out of wedlock in 1754 in Ireland. Then, the Colonel had two sons, George and James, with his wife, Katherine Monro.[12] Katherine had passed away young and the Colonel had eventually returned home to England where he was now settled.

12 University of Chicago Library, Guide to the J. Kirkpatrick Collection 1810-1811.

For James, though, it was India that was his home. Born in 1764 in Fort St. George, Madras,[13] he'd lost his mother at the tender age of eighteen months. He'd then spent many years in England, getting an education, before finally returning to Madras. He'd had his share of struggles, at times even despaired over how dim his prospects had seemed. However, his familiarity with local ways and ease with Indian languages, especially Persian, Tamil, Telegu and Hindoostani[14], proved to be an advantage for his diplomatic career with the Company and he finally replaced his half-brother William as Resident of Hyderabad.[15] He'd arrived here only recently, but admittedly, the "city of gardens" had charmed him from the very first day. Hyderabad with its regal palaces, vibrant *bazaars* and fragrant gardens! It was back in 1591 that Sultan Quli Qutb Shah had founded Hyderabad.[16] A kind and secular ruler and a wonderful administrator, he'd put his heart and soul into the planning of the city, intending it to replicate paradise itself. And it really did. Time had stripped away some of its original glory, but after Nizam Ali Khan took the throne in 1762 and subsequently shifted the capital of the Deccan from Aurangabad to Hyderabad, the city once again recovered its former opulence and grandeur.[17] The reign of Nizam Ali Khan was proving to be an extremely significant political

---

13 Lt Col James Achilles Kirkpatrick. Geni. Genealogy.

14 Interview with and research paper by Dr Aruna Pariti on "British Residency", Department of History, Osmania Women's College (Former British Residency), Hyderabad, India. February, 2022.

15 Kirkpatrick, William (1754-1812). Dictionary of National Biography, 1885-1900. U.K.

16 Interview and tour with Mr. S Anand, Registered Guide, Dept of Tourism, Govt of Telangana. January, 2022.

17 Pandharipande, Reeti and Nadimpally, Lasya. A Brief History of the Nizams of Hyderabad. *Outlook Traveller*. 5 August 2017.

period for Hyderabad. The durbar was firmly established here and regular income from the jagirs allowed the nobility to maintain very prosperous establishments. With the Nizam and the nobility being important dispensers of patronage,[18] the city continued to prosper and flourish. Now there was a magnificence, an elegance about it that James was openly and admittedly enamoured with. He thought it was ethereal, almost magical, as though the city itself was wrapped in a veil of mystical beauty.

There was the other side too, of course. The palaces, gardens and mansions were only half the story. The other half was the disease, suffering and penury, the kind that could bring loathing and distress on the faces of the most hardened men. But then, that was Hyderabad – a city of extremes. If the splendour was dazzling, then the squalor was equally distressing. If the grandeur was astounding, then the suffering was as dismal. Despite it all, James was in love with Hyderabad. It was as though there was something in the air of the city that seemed to instantly enchant, almost seduce him.

A soft knock on the door snapped him out of his thoughts.

'Come in.' He glanced at the door as it opened and his valet entered the room.

'The Pune *daak* came this morning, sir. It is on your desk.'

General Palmer, the Resident for the Maratha durbar at Pune, always sent his Calcutta despatches via Hyderabad. Palmer had been Military Secretary to Warren Hastings in the early days of his career, and had spent considerable time in the court of the Nawab Wazirs of Oudh at Lucknow before becoming Resident at Pune.

18 The Hyderabad Political System and its Participants. Karen Leonard. *The Journal of Asian Studies* Vol. 30, No. 3 (May, 1971), pp. 569-582. The Association for Asian Studies

Like James, the General had excellent linguistic skills and was well-versed with the customs and rituals of the court.[19] James was on good terms with the General and the camaraderie and transparency they shared meant that James could apprise himself on the Maratha developments before the despatches were forwarded to Calcutta.

'Thank you. I will take a look tomorrow morning.'

'Very good, sir. Would you like me to draw your bath now?'

'Yes please.' James nodded. 'And would you see that the palanquin is ready on time?'

'Certainly, sir.' Bowing slightly, the valet then walked into the marble bathroom where he busied himself for the next ten minutes. He was an efficient valet and perceptive too, so much so, that he didn't need to be told most things. Even now, he didn't ask, he simply reached out for the tiny bottle of rose oil on the side of the bathtub and tipped a few drops into the bath water. It was obvious that James needed it tonight. Perhaps it would help ease his mood.

James was feeling decidedly more relaxed when he stepped out on the portico of the bungalow that evening. December was a beautiful time in Hyderabad, and there was a definite nip in the air. Now the fragrance of the changing season combined with the *attar*[20] he had applied liberally on his neck and behind his ears, gave off a heady aroma of musk, *kesar* and cedar. The musk was particularly overpowering, but extremely popular as an essence for this traditional art of perfumery. Sniffing appreciatively, James stepped into the waiting state palanquin. The wedding was being held at the family *deorhi*, about a kilometre away from the Charminar. It

---

19 Marshall, P.J. *Eighteenth Century India. Oxford Dictionary of National Biography.* May, 2005.

20 A fragrant essential oil, typically made from rose petals.

would take the palanquin more than an hour to travel the distance. They would have to pass through the majestic old Banjara Gate and then enter the old part of the city. James was used to making the trip. Attending social events and functions was an important part of his role as a diplomat. And this wasn't just any social event. It was the wedding of a noble woman from one of Hyderabad's most influential families and would undoubtedly be a grand, opulent affair. What James wasn't aware of even as he settled into the palanquin and it set off, was that this wedding was also going to be the most monumental event of his life, one that was going to change the course of his destiny forever.

2
The Palace of The Women

Khair-un-Nissa picked up the hard-bound book from the *sheesham* table by the side of her bed. She'd been up until 3 a.m. last night, reading the last pages, but that wasn't surprising. She was an avid reader with a keen interest in poetry and literature.

Now as she walked over to the cobalt and gilt bookshelf at the end of her bedroom, Khair couldn't help glancing out of the domed window on the side. There were two zenana quarters here in her grandfather's extensive deorhi and one was exclusively for her mother, sister and her, while the other was occupied by her grandmother, Durdana Begum. The deorhi was not far from the Charminar, in a lane behind a famous, bustling bazaar, but Khair had little to do with all that. The entrance which led into the women's quarters was a separate one and Khair lived in a protected world of uniformed, armed women guards and enormous double gates which were imposing enough to keep the world out.

'Seems like the whole world has been invited today,' murmured Khair to herself, as she peered out of the window. Despite the fact that the zenana mansion was at the rear of the main deorhi, from this window she had an excellent view of the fountains and fruit trees below, as well as the city sights beyond. Right now, though, her eyes were riveted on the gardens. If they looked splendid on an ordinary day, then today there was an undeniable magnificence about them, as there was about the mansion itself. The crystal chandeliers had been polished, the gardens trimmed to perfection, the fairy lights strung everywhere. After all, it was the wedding of Nazir-un-Nissa, the older granddaughter.[21] Not surprisingly, the grounds below were already coming alive with the throngs of people who were pouring in for the wedding. But here, in Khair's private quarters, all was quiet.

'What is it about?' Just then, her older cousin walked into the room and closed the door behind her. 'Love?' She gestured toward the book in Khair's hand.

Love. A single word, but it intrigued Khair.

She didn't quite know what it was though. How could she?

Slipping the book back into the bookcase, Khair joined her cousin on the velvet *divan*. 'Yes. The daughter of a rich landowner falls in love with a destitute peasant.'

'Who cannot afford to feed her more than a single bowl of rice and lentils every day,' concluded her cousin. 'Impossible!' She dismissed it with a quick wave of her hand. 'Two opposite worlds can never meet.'

'They might,' Khair insisted then. 'After all, it is love! Nothing is impossible in love.'

'You are too naïve.' Shifting a little, the older girl came closer to Khair. 'There was a mehfil at one of the minister's houses last week, with dance performances and poetry recitations that went on well into the morning. Chanda Bibi performed too.'

Khair had heard of the celebrated courtesan of course, the one who was not only a talented singer and dancer, but a wonderful

21 Nazir-un-Nissa. Geni. Genealogy.

poet as well. Chanda Bibi had been born to a courtesan named Raj Kunwar, and Bahadur Khan, a *mansabdar* at the Mughal emperor Muhammad Shah's court. Despite not belonging to a royal family, Chanda Bibi had received an aristocratic upbringing and had been well educated in arts and aesthetics. A master at the unique Deccani *Kathak* style of dance, she had been trained in *thumri* by Khushhal Khan, the great-grandson of Tansen.[22] She trained other courtesans at her palace and was also well accomplished in the skills of horse riding, hunting and archery.[23]

'Do you know she is among the first women to have authored and compiled a *diwan*[24] of *ghazals?*' remarked Khair's cousin. Smiling, she poured herself a glass of rose and almond sherbet from the silver *surahi* on the table.

'I have heard she is quite a favourite of the Nizam,' said Khair.

'Yes, he holds her in high esteem.' Khair's cousin nodded. 'In fact, it is common knowledge that she has several admirers, including the Prime Minister and even his Private Secretary. But then, it is hardly surprising. After all, she is easily one of the most beautiful and accomplished women in the city. Her dance is sublime, as are her ghazals.'

Khair looked visibly impressed and her cousin laughed. 'Speaking of ghazals, you should hear some of the poetry that is recited in these mehfils. But I suppose you are much too young and naïve for all that. Perhaps that is why you believe anything is possible in love.'

---

22 Thathipalli, Mallik. The moon-cheeked poet and her forgotten legacy. *The Hindu. Business Line.* March 29th, 2021.

23 Stewart, Courtney, A. *Feminine Power of the Deccan.* The Metropolitan Museum of Art, New York. Dept of Islamic Art.

24 Interview with Rana Safvi. Historian and Writer. May, 2022.

Khair shrugged, in that nonchalant way that young people often do. 'I suppose you are right. Love does not really exist, does it? Only in books and music and poetry.'

'Oh, that is not always love.' Her cousin giggled and then looked at Khair conspiratorially. 'There is also lust, my dear Khair.'

Khair sighed. As if love wasn't confusing enough, now there was also lust to think about. 'I suppose the two are related,' she suggested meekly.

'Sometimes. But not necessarily. Nevertheless, neither of them is usually the basis for marriage, are they?'

That was true. Love marriages weren't really the norm in Hyderabad. In fact, far from it. And it wasn't only Hyderabad. Khair had heard from the wives and daughters of foreign diplomats who visited the deorhi, that even in the West, love wasn't the basis for marriage. In fact, that was one thing that even the most culturally diverse societies seemed to have in common. Marriages were more like contracts where convenience and reciprocity were the motivators. Khair, even with her limited understanding, couldn't comprehend why love wasn't the "be all and end all" of all relationships and life. After all, wasn't it constantly showed off, flaunted at parties and mehfils and symposia? Weren't the greatest literary works all based on love? Even all the poets and dancers and artists couldn't stop obsessing about it. You'd think then, wouldn't you, that it should have been deemed the finest, most supreme emotion? And yet, time and again it had been disgraced, shamed, condemned as an irrational thing, a sensation sometimes even equated with a sort of absurd madness, a lunacy which had been responsible for the ruin of many.

'Ya Allah! You should see the look on your face, dear Khair!' The older girl suddenly giggled and then nudged her. 'Anyone would think you were in love yourself.'

'And if I was?' Khair looked up to meet her cousin's eyes. Her gaze was steadfast and her face had suddenly taken on a rather determined expression. At times like these, she looked like a mirror image of her mother.

The velvet divan was a spacious three-seater, but the two girls were sitting so close to one another that their shoulders were almost touching. Her lower lip quivering with anticipation at this sudden announcement, the older girl bent in even closer to Khair. 'Really? How? And...where? I mean...who is he Khair? How could you...?'

'Why not?' The determined look had now acquired a tenor of stubbornness.

'Because love...love can ruin. It can destroy everything. It is ruthless and...'

'As the great poet, Saadi Shirazi once said, *the rose and the thorn, and sorrow and gladness are linked together.* Do you not agree, my dear cousin? After all, Saadi Shirazi was a great man and a remarkable preacher.'

'Yes, of course, but love? Khair really...'

'Ya Allah! Now it is your turn to see the look on your face!' Smiling, Khair leaned back into the soft contours of the divan. 'You really did believe me, did you not? Thought I was madly in love with someone wildly inappropriate, thus wreaking havoc on the family honour.'

'Khair!' Smacking her gently on the hand, her cousin shook her head. 'Sometimes I worry about you. Really, what is to become of you?'

'Worry about yourself for once, dear cousin.' Khair tilted her head slightly and pointed to the wall-mounted pendulum clock above the carved, domed bed. 'It is almost time and you are not even dressed yet.'

Looking suddenly panicked, her cousin's eyes flew in the direction of the clock. Realizing how late it was, she hurriedly rose from the divan. 'You are right, I should go! I have to change and it is almost time.' She glanced at Khair then. 'Are you not coming down?'

'In a while. I am almost ready and there is still a little time.'

She watched her cousin hurry across the room and close the ornate double doors behind her as she stepped out. Khair shook her head, thinking about the conversation they'd just had. 'Look at me, obsessing over something that does not even concern me,' she murmured to herself then. 'After all, I have not even met the man I am to marry.'

This was of course, very common. The betel leaf had been given, but all Khair knew about the young man she was betrothed to, was that he was of aristocratic descent and generally considered "perfectly suitable" for her. The fact that a girl as young as Khair was already engaged to be married, was also not unusual. It was common practice, in fact.[25] The match had been arranged by her maternal grandfather, Baqar-Ali-Khan. That however, was actually rare. But then their circumstances were different. Khair's father, Mehdi Yar Khan, had passed away many years ago.[26] Khair and her sister had therefore been brought up in their maternal grandfather's home. A congenial old man from a Persian family of scholars, Baqar-Ali-

---

25 Interview with Dr Shankar Kumar. Noted Historian. Hindu College, Delhi University. Dec, 2021.

26 Mehdi Yar Khan. Geni. Genealogy.

Khan had come to India from Iran many years ago and was now a high-ranking official in the Nizam's army. His cousin was the Prime Minister's Private Secretary and their family was one of the most influential ones in Hyderabad.

Having lived all her life in the family deorhi, it was not surprising that Khair-un-Nissa was well-versed with the way things were done in their sect. They were *Sayyids* after all, direct descendants of the Prophet himself.[27] Needless to say, the austere rules that governed their clan were unquestioningly followed by all, particularly when it came to delicate subjects like marriage. The strange thing was that Khair was also inwardly well-aware that if she chose to object to the match, she would have had her mother's support. That wasn't always common, particularly in their sect, but her mother was different. Intelligent, skilful and with a fearless determination, Sharaf-un-Nissa was, despite the shackles of conservative customs and boundaries that were intrinsic in their society, a progressive and free-thinking woman. Sometimes it was unbelievable to Khair, the way her mother was. She didn't seem at all daunted or bound by the traditions that were staunchly followed by everyone else around her.

Smiling to herself, Khair rose from the divan and reached for her gold-threaded, chiffon *dupatta.* Her bangles made a tinkling sound as she picked it up. This one wasn't quite six yards long like the one that her sister would be wearing tonight – the *khada dupatta.*[28] A stiff, heavily embellished drape, it was evident why a bride found it

---

27 Interview with and research paper by Dr Aruna Pariti on "British Residency", Department of History, Osmania Women's College (Former British Residency), Hyderabad, India. February, 2022.

28 Ali, Nayare. Drapes from Royalty. *Deccan Chronicle.* 17 May 2018.

difficult to smile while wearing one. But then, it was tradition and a Hyderabadi bride was inconceivable without it, for it was a sign that a girl has now become a woman.

Careful not to leave even a single strand of her dark hair uncovered, Khair draped her dupatta over her head. Her delicate hands then moved over the bodice of her long, bejewelled *zardozi* kurta, expertly smoothening out the creases as she simultaneously turned toward the gilded mirror in front of her. The emerald and pearl *chokar, chandbalis,* bangles, *bajuband* and *jhoomar*[29] were spectacular, but Khair looked just as lovely without them as well. She was a naturally beautiful young woman with a quiet elegance about her that stood out on its own. Now as she looked into the mirror, the dark brown, kohl-lined eyes that stared back at her were intense, strong, resilient. They were the eyes of a young woman who saw, understood, comprehended, sometimes far more than her not so advanced years let on. The eyes that sometimes looked as though they could take in the world and it still wouldn't be enough. Just like the woman they belonged to.

Khair closed her eyes. Raising her right hand, she gently placed it on the left side of her chest, just below her collar bone. Yes, she could feel it clearly, the strange, rapid beating of her heart. The easy banter she had shared with her cousin a while ago had been enjoyable, but Khair's attempt at levity had also been her effort to try and quell this feeling that she'd been experiencing since the morning. But why? She'd never felt like this before, this...this inexplicable, unsettled sense. With a keenness of spirit and a thirst to experience the new, she'd always had a naturally curious mind that urged her, propelled

29 Women in Deccani Painting. Select artworks from the collection of Salar Jung Museum, Hyderabad, India. Google Arts and Culture.

her to explore, imagine and wonder. Of course, Khair had learnt to contain her dreams, her imagination, her yearnings, well within the austere laws that had always governed her life. She knew the rules and she'd learnt to live by them. Time and again, her heart and her mind had tried to wander, stray, drift, but she'd always managed to rein them in. But today, something was different. Something felt different. It was almost as if there was something in the air today, something strange that was pulling at her, luring her, tempting her. As though the winds themselves were whispering to her, giving their secrets out to her. She couldn't understand it though, couldn't fathom, couldn't comprehend, for today, her thoughts seemed to be a thousand worlds away. But was it her heart or her mind that was speaking to her? She couldn't tell.

The pendulum clock suddenly chimed out and Khair's eyes snapped open. Drawing her hand away from her chest, she smacked herself lightly on the forehead and then broke into peals of laughter, suddenly looking like the very young girl that she was, the contemplative look instantly gone. 'What is wrong with me? Standing here by myself, musing away. I am going to be late if I do not hurry now.'

She quickly checked her reflection one last time, adjusted her dupatta and stepped away from the mirror. Then as fast as her long, heavily embellished outfit would allow, she walked to the double doors, pulled them open and stepped out of the room, eager to join the wedding revelries downstairs.

3
Collision of Two Worlds

The sun was just starting its slow descent into the calm waters of the Musi and the fragrance of attar, perfumed water and rose flowers hung heavy in the air when James's palanquin came to a halt outside the mansion. Even as he got out and headed toward the entrance, he could see that the wedding party was still at the gates. The groom, dressed in a heavily embellished jama and churidar, was sitting atop a bejewelled white horse, clutching the reins in his hennaed hands. The *sehra*[30] that covered the front of his face was encrusted with gemstones and he was wearing a pearl and emerald *satlada*[31] around his neck. Dozens of men dressed in traditional Indian dress of the finest fabrics followed him, some on horses, some on elephants and others on foot. Inside the mansion, the scene was just as opulent. The pre-wedding rituals had gone on until the wee hours of the morning, but there was not the slightest tiredness on anyone's face today. After all, elaborate, extravagant ceremonies were an intrinsic part of any Hyderabadi wedding. The actual *nikah* of course was a simple ceremony that would be conducted by the *imam* late at night, but the celebrations usually went on for several

30 A Sehra is a head-dress worn by the groom during Indian, Pakistani and Bangladeshi weddings.

31 Satlada is a seven-stringed pearl necklace of Indian origin.

days, sometimes weeks. Today, to a spectator, the mansion itself looked like a bride, strung with millions of minuscule fairy lights in a glittering rainbow of colours. Outside, in the sprawling central courtyard, a *shamiana* had been set up and turbaned servers with silver trays were proffering *paan,* fruits and Syrah to the guests. Hundreds of people had been invited which was evident from the length of the white *dastarkhwan*[32] laid out in the main hall. A variety of meats done to perfection in the *tandoor,* perfectly spiced curries, breads, *biryanis, haleem,* pickles, saffron and rose flavoured desserts garnished with gold and silver foil, heart-shaped betel leaves and all kinds of exotic fruits were on the menu that night. It was going to be a feast that would be talked about and a wedding that would be remembered for years.

To someone else, the sheer magnificence and grandeur of such a vision would have seemed astounding, but James had witnessed such social events many a time, and he didn't even bat an eyelid as he strode into the central courtyard, his arms laden with gifts. It was customary to present the bride and her family with clothes and jewellery and James understood the traditions of Hyderabadi society well. As he stopped to greet friends and make small talk with acquaintances, it was actually difficult to believe that this handsome, tall man with his perfectly accented Persian and flawless Indian mannerisms was not a born and bred Hyderabadi nobleman.[33] Accepting a glass of Syrah from a passing server, James disappeared into the milling crowd.

---

32 Interview with Salma Yusuf Hussain. Food Historian and Persian Scholar. May, 2022.

33 Interview with Dr Shankar Kumar. Noted Historian. Hindu College, Delhi University. Dec, 2021.

Soon, the central courtyard and the main hall in the mansion were both alive with sounds of laughter and animated conversation. James, looking regal in his purple jama, was standing in the middle of a large group of ministers. The conversation was centred around local politics, usually a favoured subject with James. Today, however, despite the excellent company, he was finding it difficult to concentrate on anything. The previous feeling of restiveness had returned and his mind was agitated once more.

'Hushmat Jung is looking distracted today.' One of the ministers to the Nizam's durbar laughed. 'Is everything all right?'

James smiled at the use of this title that the Nizam had bestowed on him, Hushmat Jung[34] – Valiant in battle.

'Then he must certainly try the *Baghaar-e-Baingan*[35],' remarked Mir Alam with a smile. 'We all know his fondness for it.' A slight man with an unusually sharp, observant face, Mir Alam was Baqar-Ali-Khan's first cousin and Prime Minister Aristu Jah's private secretary. He was known to have come from the *Nuriya Syeds* of Shustar in Persia and his family was acclaimed for their contributions to Islamic literature. Mir Alam's father, a famous scholar, had migrated to India as a young man and settled down in Hyderabad. It had been tradition for him to pay a visit to the Nizam every Tuesday and recommend an individual for his patronage.[36] His oldest son, Saiyed Abdul Qasim, was born in 1752 in Irani Gully, a short distance from the Charminar. Ruthlessly ambitious as also well regarded for his education and intelligence, he had done

34 Ali Khan, Raza. *Hyderabad 400 Years.* Hyderabad: Zenith Services, 1991.

35 Baghāre baingan is a curry from the Hyderabadi cuisine made with eggplant.

36 Prakash, Dr. Satya *An Outline of Ancestral History of Salar Jungs.* Hyderabad: Published by The Salar Jung Museum.

very well and now was second only to Aristu Jah in matters of the Nizam's durbar. The title of Mir Alam[37] had been bestowed on him as a gesture of appreciation and respect.

'I agree! After all, we had it made especially for you.' The grandfather of the bride, Baqar-Ali-Khan, joined the group.

James stepped forward to greet him immediately. He couldn't help noticing that unlike Mir Alam, Baqar-Ali-Khan's smile reached his eyes every time.

'Thank you.' James placed his right hand on his heart and bowed slightly, showing his appreciation. For most people who came to Hyderabad, the Hyderabadi biryani was the most delightful culinary experience. For James, however, it was the Baghaar-e-Baingan that really did make his heart sing. Everyone knew his fondness for it.[38]

'You have been very generous Hushmat Jung.' Baqar-Ali-Khan indicated the pile of presents that James had brought. 'Why do you not accompany me to the zenana and present them to the ladies yourself?'

For a moment, James wondered whether he'd heard correctly. It was common knowledge that the women in Baqar-Ali-Khan's deorhi never entered the main mansion, always staying within the luxurious confines of the women's quarters. James, of course, was no stranger to this. After all, he was well-versed with the rules and etiquette of aristocratic Hyderabadi society and had a zenana of his own at the Residency as well. Men rarely, if ever, visited the zenanas and that too only for a very valid reason, such as a medical

---

37 Nanisetti, Sarish. Mir Alam Bahadur is remembered for his gifts to Hyderabad. *The Hindu.* 30 March, 2019.

38 Banerji, Chitrita. *Eating India – Exploring the Food and Culture of the Land of Spices.* India: Bloomsbury Press, 2009.

emergency or an urgent legal matter. Then too, they were closely watched by an appointed chaperone and the women would usually converse with the visitor from behind a curtain or lattice.

'I am sorry?' James looked at the old man, a puzzled, hesitant smile on his face.

'And they say I am hard of hearing.' Baqar-Ali-Khan laughed heartily and patted James on the back. 'You are my good friend, are you not? Yes, it would be a matter of pride for me if you were to accompany me to the zenana and present these gifts to my wife and daughter yourself,' he repeated then.

James was admittedly touched. The invitation was a clear indicator that Baqar-Ali-Khan considered him to be a valued friend and trusted brother. It was a definite mark of respect.

'It would be my honour.' James smiled warmly at the older man and together, they made their way across the hall, through the outer courtyard and toward the rear of the mansion.

The architectural style of the zenana was the same as the main mansion, with a domination of European, Persian and Indian influences. Opulent and elegant, it was decorated with an abundance of intricate stucco work, marble arches, latticed windows, carved verandas, porticos and domes. In the centre of the ground floor, directly facing the courtyard, lay the banquet hall adorned with expensive Persian carpets in rich colours, white and gold furniture with hand-carved motif work and gleaming crystal chandeliers. A winding marble staircase led up to the first and second floors and some of the verandas looked over smaller courtyards and flower gardens where the ladies could spend languid afternoons or evenings, sipping sherbet and playing cards.

'Please.' Baqar-Ali-Khan waved James into a carved armchair in the banquet hall. Just like the main mansion, here too, the revelries were on in full swing. 'My wife and daughter will be here in a few moments.'

'Sherbet, sahib?'

Even though he'd already had two glasses of Syrah at the main mansion, James knew it would have been rude to refuse. Smiling, he nodded and reached out his hand for a glass of the ruby rose sherbet. As he lifted the glass from the silver tray that was being proffered to him, he suddenly sensed a movement from across the hall. Distracted, James turned. Other than the carved double doors at the entrance, this room had eight arched windows and two domed doors which led to the flower gardens outside. The movement had come from the domed door on the right. His arm still outstretched, as though suspended in mid-air, James watched as a tassled silk curtain was slowly, deliberately, drawn apart and a pair of dark brown, kohled eyes appeared. At first, only the eyes were visible and then slowly, inch by inch, the lovely face behind the curtain was revealed. The shimmering chandbali that hung from her dainty earlobe was spectacular, but it was her eyes that had him transfixed. There was a spark in them, like a quiet fire that seemed to instantly ignite something deep within him, as though all his dormant longings had stirred and awakened. Even as he stood there staring, James noticed that a single strand of dark hair seemed to have somehow escaped the dupatta that had been tightly wrapped around her head, and he had a sudden desire to reach out and tuck it behind her ear. And then, he saw it. It was small, almost indiscernible from the distance that separated them, but somehow, still impossible to miss. The tiny beauty mark just above her chin that told him that it really was *her*. Khair-un-Nissa. The young lady he had heard so much about. And she was beautiful, so beautiful in fact, that if anyone had asked him to describe her, he wouldn't have been able to do it, for no words would have done justice. James continued to stare, as though he was in a trance. She was still peeking out furtively from behind the curtain, those dark, animated eyes darting from left to right and then back again, as she took in the scene around her. And then suddenly, the movement stopped. Their eyes locked and time stood still. The sounds, the voices, the laughter, everything around them seemed to dissipate as James and Khair looked at each other for the very first time. And as they stood there, several feet apart, separated by throngs of talking, laughing women and a half drawn, tassled silk curtain, something took over both of them, something far beyond any semblance of practicality or realization of the boundaries that had always governed their two very different lives. It was strange, inexplicable, iike something that neither of them had ever experienced before. As though rain was pouring down from an otherwise clear sky. Or torrential waves crashing on the shores of a calm sea. It was almost as if today, right now, right here, the world was just beginning and anything was possible, even the unimaginable. And as they stood there, looking at each other, they both instantly knew that this was real. This was fate, destiny, providence. This was true.

This was love.

4
The Dilemma and the Decision

Not surprisingly, he did dream about her that night. It was a moving dream though, with the Charminar appearing and disappearing in the background and the sky rapidly changing moods from calm to stormy and then calm again. The only thing that remained unchanged and constant was the lady herself, Khair-un-Nissa. The one with the beautiful kohled eyes and that reticent smile that had etched itself so firmly in James's mind that he hadn't been able to stop thinking about it.

It had seemed like hours that they'd stood there, rooted to the spot, looking at each other. At first they'd simply stared, almost unblinkingly. In fact, it had even seemed like that game that James had often played with his brother when they'd been children – Who blinks first? It had gone on like that for a while and then, without warning, she'd broken the spell with a sudden, hesitant half-smile. *"When I saw you, I fell in love, and you smiled because you knew."* Perfectly appropriate to the situation, the famous quote by Shakespeare had fleetingly passed through his mind and it was at that moment that James had realized that his arm was still suspended in mid-air, holding the silver tumbler filled to the brim with rose sherbet. He'd withdrawn his arm then and even as she watched him, still half-hidden behind the curtain, he'd lifted the glass to his lips and sipped. His eyes had stayed riveted on her. It was only when he'd finally heard footsteps right behind him that he'd snapped out of his trance-like state. And just like that, they both blinked, the curtain was hastily drawn again and the room had come back into focus.

Everything else after that remained a haze. Baqar-Ali-Khan walking up to him, accompanied by two ladies. He introduced the older lady as his wife, Durdana Begum and the younger one as his daughter, Sharaf-un-Nissa. Despite his extremely distracted state-of-mind, James had established that the younger woman was Khair-un-Nissa's mother. Then, pleasantries were exchanged, congratulations offered. James presented the wedding gifts to them and they accepted graciously. Later, the old gentleman and he walked back to the main mansion and resumed drinking Syrah and conversing with the other men. But none of it had seemed real to James. The only thing that had any sense of reality for him was the beautiful young lady he had seen behind the silk curtain. It was almost as though all his senses had suddenly awakened, as though hundreds of questions had been answered with the utmost clarity in a single instant and now he could see, hear and understand everything more lucidly than he'd ever been able to do.

Having spent a fitful night, tossing and turning in his four-poster bed, James awoke feeling tired the next morning. He'd thought the feeling of restiveness he'd been experiencing the previous day would dissipate on its own, but now it seemed to have settled more firmly inside him. Trying to ignore it, he had his usual *Chhota Hazri*, comprising of a cup of tea and a piece of fruit, served to him in bed.[39] It was however only when he had settled down at his desk after a

39 Garodia Gupta, Archana. *Food in British India. The Indian Express.* 20 December 2018.

more substantial breakfast of devilled kidneys on toast, that he felt inclined to shift his attention to the paperwork on his table. He'd already opened the Pune daak earlier that morning, but there was a letter from his half-brother William that he still had to attend to. James and William often exchanged letters to apprise each other about official developments, and also as an outlet for expressing their feelings and thoughts to each other. Obviously, since William was Military Secretary to the Governor General in Calcutta, this informal correspondence was strategically significant to James.[40]

James reached for his sterling silver paper knife and slit open the envelope. Even as he did so, a small smile started playing on his lips. Other than being fond of his half-brother, James was admittedly also proud of William's achievements. William's sharp mind and linguistic capabilities had ensured his success in his military and diplomatic career with the Company. He had been the Persian interpreter for Lieutenant General Giles Stibbert before assuming the position of Resident at Gwalior. He had also been Persian Interpreter for Lord Cornwallis in the Mysore War of 1790, and then had been sent to Nayakote for a mission in 1793. William had been among the first Englishmen to cross the towering mountains of the region and Lord Cornwallis had later remarked that nobody else could have accomplished the mission with the kind of alertness and discretion that William had shown. Then in 1795, he had taken over the position of Resident of Hyderabad. His health though hadn't cooperated and he had to move to the Cape where he met

---

40 Wilkinson, Callie Hannah. Dissertation on "The Residents of the British East India Company at Indian Royal Courts" c. 1798-1818. Wolfson College. University of Cambridge. July, 2017.

Lord Wellesley and finally accompanied him to Calcutta to assume the position of Military Secretary.[41]

Pulling out the letter, James quickly scanned its contents. It was mostly official, though the usual enquiry about Dhoolaury Bibi was there as well. The relationship that his brother shared with his Indian mistress had an intimate quality to it that had clearly been missing in his marriage with Maria Pawson. James was aware of how deeply William cared about Dhoolaury and he could easily envision the two of them settling into a comfortable life in the future.

Ten minutes later, as he was writing out a response to William, the thought did cross James's mind that transparent though their relationship was in many other ways, he could not even contemplate mentioning the events of the previous evening to his brother. James didn't think that William would understand. How could he? After all, James himself didn't completely understand it.

He put the quill down and massaged his right temple with his thumb and forefinger. Admittedly, he was bemused. It wasn't as though these things hadn't happened before; plenty of officers lived with local women and even maintained their own harems.[42] Of course, attitudes were becoming more prejudiced than they used to be, but it still wasn't an extraordinary situation. But Khair-un-Nissa, now she certainly was extraordinary. In fact, the most extraordinary woman he had ever seen. And of course, the fact that she belonged to one of the most influential, noble families in Hyderabad, made the situation that much more complicated. Besides, she was already engaged to someone else.[43] Their

---

41 Kirkpatrick, William (1754-1812). Dictionary of National Biography, 1885-1900. U.K.

42 Interview with Rana Safvi. Historian and Writer. May, 2022.

43 Interview with Dr Shankar Kumar. Noted Historian. Hindu College, Delhi University. Dec, 2021.

worlds were as different, as they could have been, where was the meeting point? But what meeting point was he even looking for? He couldn't marry the lady, that much was certain. The thought was outrageous, impossible and...yes, admittedly, dangerous. As mesmerized as James had been by her last night, now, in the clear light of day, there was no way that he could deny the perils of the situation. Shaking his head, as though trying to drive away all thoughts of her, he picked up the quill again and resumed writing the letter.

The situation on the other side of the city was, however, different. The wedding ceremonies had been on all night, but unlike James, Khair hadn't even gone to bed. She knew sleep would be elusive and so, still dressed in her heavily embellished outfit, she'd spent the early morning hours in her favourite sheesham armchair, staring out of her bedroom window. Try as she might, she just couldn't get the handsome, tall British officer out of her mind. She played and replayed the scene a hundred times in her head, the way they'd looked at each other, his arm outstretched, almost as though he was reaching out to her. To her own astonishment, she found herself wondering what it would have felt like to touch that graceful hand with its long elegant fingers, to feel them threading their way through her dark hair, tracing a line down her cheek. The thought was outrageous, but the feeling seemed to engulf her, surround her, besiege her, until the longing was almost too much for her to bear. Khair shifted restlessly in her chair and looked up at the sky. There was still some time for sunrise, but the first of the pre-dawn light had already appeared, slowly stretching its arms across the skyline, splashing the horizon with streaks of magenta pink. In the distance, coming gradually into focus was the heart of the city, the Charminar. Built in 1591 by Muhammad Quli Qutb Shah, the Charminar had four arches, four main minars and four entrance arches in four directions. The magic of four![44] Khair had always thought that there was something complete, flawless, about it. Legend had it that there had been a plague that had spread like wildfire in the city back then and the king had built the Charminar as an offering to god. The lotus in the centre ceiling was a motif of the Quli Qutb Shahi kings and effigies of pigeons, parrots, squirrels and peacocks could be found everywhere in the delicate stucco work.[45] Now the creamy colour of the beautiful limestone structure seemed to radiate an almost ethereal luminescence at this hour. Soon the sun would emerge from its resting place and the horizon would once again be a vast expanse of deep blue, as blue as the handsome Englishman's eyes. Khair sighed! Those eyes... They were like the sky itself. Endless, limitless, boundless. So much so, that she could have immersed herself in them. Deeper and deeper. More and more. Completely, entirely, absolutely, until the time that she was one with them.

'If this is not love, I do not know what is!' she suddenly exclaimed, her clear voice ringing through the silence of her bedroom. It was almost as if she'd needed to say it out loud to believe it. Khair shook her head as though banishing all uncertainties, all hesitations, all fears from her mind. 'She should talk to me about love now,' she said to herself then, thinking about the conversation she'd had only a few hours earlier with her cousin. 'Impossible, did she say? Far-fetched,

44 Interview with Mr. M.A. Qayyum, Historian and Former Deputy Director, Department of Archaeology and Museums, Hyderabad. March, 2022.

45 Interview and tour with Mr. S Anand, Registered Guide, Dept of Tourism, Govt of Telangana. January, 2022.

was it? Did I not tell her that when it comes to love, nothing is ever impossible, nothing far-fetched!' Smiling broadly, the young girl jumped up from the armchair and ran to the door before she could change her mind. So maybe she was being impulsive and irrational. But then, wasn't that what love was anyway? Impulsive, irrational, outrageous! Flinging open the doors, she ran down the corridor, all the way to the far end, her delicate silver anklets making a tinkling sound as she went. She needed to share this moment with someone, and who else but the person who understood her the most. The one person who had always given Khair the courage to follow her dreams, her heart. Her mother, Sharaf-un-Nissa.

Exhausted after the elaborate wedding ceremonies, Sharaf-un-Nissa had fallen into a deep slumber just a couple of hours before the frantic banging on her door awakened her with a start. Thinking that surely somebody must be gravely sick, she had rushed to the door, only to find her younger daughter standing there, still dressed in the clothes she had worn for the wedding. Astonished and worried, she then ushered Khair into the room. Two minutes later, mother and daughter were sitting down in Sharaf-un-Nissa's private sitting room, the first glimpses of the early morning light filtering in through the sheer silk curtains. Usually when Sharaf-un-Nissa entertained her daughters here in her private quarters, she unfailingly offered them a beverage. Tea was the popular choice during the winter months while a fruit-based sherbet was preferred during the hotter season. Today, however, neither did Sharaf-un-Nissa remember to offer, not did Khair notice. With her heart desperately urging her toward the path it had chosen for her, food and drink were the last things on her mind. Now, without waiting for her mother to ask, Khair started talking. As always, there was no hesitation, no reluctance, nothing omitted. Within mere minutes, she had poured everything out to the older woman, who for her part, had listened to her daughter without a single interruption.

Once she had finished, Khair searched her mother's face, trying to fathom her thoughts. Her heavily kohled eyes half-closed, her perfectly arched brows furrowed in concentration, Sharaf-un-Nissa seemed to be deep in thought as Khair watched her. 'Atleast she does not look furious,' murmured Khair to herself then. 'Perhaps not even upset.'

'Hmmm... So, you think you are in love, my little one.' At last, her mother broke the silence and looked at Khair quizzically.

'I am in love,' Khair said softly then. The emphasis on the word "am" was clear.

This time her mother smiled at her. 'Hushmat Jung,' she said then with a slow nod. 'A handsome and powerful man.' She cocked her head to one side and stroked her chin thoughtfully. 'The Nizam himself is very fond of him. As is the Prime Minister. Yes, it is a good match. Inshallah, a very good match.'

Admittedly, Khair was shocked. She knew that compared to the others, her mother was a free-thinking woman. She also knew that plenty of Indian women had married senior British officers and many of those marriages had been very successful as well. But this was different. After all, they were Sayyids and never married outside the confines of their sect. This was, in mild words, sacrilege!

Sharaf-un-Nissa had noticed her daughter's bemused face and as though reading her thoughts, she now leaned forward and patted her on the hand. 'I am proud of you, Khair *Joon*. You have chosen well.'

Khair smiled tentatively, still not completely able to understand her mother's ready acceptance. 'What about my engagement?' she asked then. Even talking about it now made her recoil, but the question was inevitable and had to be asked. 'Everything has already been fixed.'

'I always knew it was an unsuitable alliance. You deserve so much better.' Sharaf-un-Nissa dismissed the question with a wave of her hand.

'But what about *Nana*? He will never accept this and...'

'Do not worry about him.' Her mother cut her off this time. 'He never should have got involved in this. It is not his responsibility.' Her voice was firm and resolute.

Rising from the divan, she then walked over to where Khair was sitting. Bending down, she kissed her daughter on the forehead, as though bestowing a blessing. 'You have chosen well, Khair Joon,' she repeated. 'Leave the rest to me.'

'Thank you *Maman* Joon.' The younger woman breathed a sigh of relief. Her mother had always been her closest confidante and now she understood why. With her extraordinary courage and determination, she exuded confidence.

'Now, would you like a cup of chai?' Sharaf-un-Nissa smiled at Khair. 'It is much too late to go to bed. Though I suspect, you will not be able to sleep even if you try. Am I correct?'

Khair nodded and leaned her head against her mother's bosom. 'A cup of chai would certainly be nice.'

Five minutes later, a maid brought in two steaming cups of the spiced black tea, garnished with pods of green cardamom and fragrant saffron threads. Then mother and daughter settled down in the comfortable divan to watch the sunrise together.

5
Midst of Moonflowers

Several days had passed since that first sighting. Strange days, they had been too. Admittedly, he'd gone through a multitude of emotions. It was a revelation one moment and then the deepest sense of regret the next. Utter despair over letting something precious tumble out of his hands one moment, and firm, resolute conviction the next. Sometimes he even saw visions, heard sounds. Then he'd shake his head as he tried to drive away the shimmer of that chandbali or the tinkle of those bangles. He'd consciously try not to think about what it would be like to touch that tiny beauty mark above her chin or tuck that stray strand of hair behind her ear. Even as these thoughts crossed his mind, James would then admonish himself for being irrational and impulsive. 'This is madness', he'd tell himself firmly. 'I must be going barmy or something, fantasizing like this. I really need to pull myself together.' Despite that, James couldn't deny, at least not to himself, that he was most certainly intrigued by Khair-un-Nissa. Forgetting her was not going to be easy. If it was at all possible.

Thankfully for James, there was a lot happening on the official front and that provided a much-needed diversion. Lord Wellesley had always been an ambitious man, but many believed that he was also influenced by the political aspirations of William Pitt, the Younger.[46] Whether it was a goal to compensate for the loss of American colonies or wipe out the influence of the French, both Pitt and Wellesley were candidly aggressive in their approach to control India. Of course, like several other British officers, Wellesley too thought of colonial cities as planned and structured and their inhabitants civilized. On the other hand, he saw Indian cities as unstructured and disorderly, with inhabitants who needed to be taught and disciplined. It was no wonder then, that Wellesley was naturally inclined toward aggressive strategies in his quest to expand British control in the subcontinent.[47] From a personal viewpoint, his attitude wasn't one that James agreed with since forceful, antagonistic tactics weren't the kind that James liked to employ, particularly when it came to the country he loved so much. Of course, he didn't voice his inner feelings to the Governor General who now seemed to have very precise, very well-defined targets. The result was that the attention was now on the acquisition of India and on a much more specific target in the short term. The object of the Governor General's current fixation was actually, no secret. Therefore, it was hardly surprising to anyone when the British finally declared war on Tipu Sultan, the fourth war between the East India Company and the Kingdom of Mysore.

A skilled negotiator and strategist, James had always taken his diplomatic responsibility very seriously and had successfully maintained a steadfastly good relationship between the Company and the Nizam. However, with this war now well underway, James

46 Giddings, Robert. *Imperial Echoes: Eye Witness Accounts of Victoria's Little Wars.* Great Britain. Leó Cooper. An Imprint of Pen & Sword Books Ltd. Great Britain. 1996.

47 Campbell, Ryan. La Salle University. *The Histories. Richard Wellesley and the Fourth Anglo Mysore War.* Volume 15, Issue 1. 2019.

was aware that his role was going to become more crucial than ever before.

He was in his study, poring over some urgent paperwork late one evening when his butler knocked on the door to announce the arrival of some ladies from Baqar-Ali-Khan's zenana. Now this wasn't the first time James had received visitors from his older friend's palace. In fact, visitors from the old part of the city often stopped by and were always warmly welcomed at the Residency. James was also well-aware that the visit could be a perfectly ordinary one and might mean nothing at all. Then again, he couldn't deny the possibility that it could mean everything.

'They are having tea at the zenana,' said the butler referring to James's own women's quarters. 'Durdana Begum, her daughter and three younger ladies.'

'Thank you.' Not the slightest emotion crossed his face as he nodded slightly, acknowledging the information. In his work, he had learned to be poker-faced. It came so effortlessly to him that it was almost second nature. Even now, his expression gave nothing away, nor did his tone when he thanked the butler and then turned back to his papers. His heart though was another matter. James was just glad that the door where the butler was standing was at too much of a distance for the man to hear the frantic, almost audibly painful beating of his heart that was now throbbing inside his chest like a wild thing.

Durdana Begum and her daughter, Sharaf-un-Nissa. Khair's grandmother and mother. Was Khair with them too? The butler hadn't said and obviously, James hadn't asked. But he didn't have to. He knew. With the utmost certainty. She was there.

Over the next hour, he found it almost impossible to concentrate on work. In fact, just the knowledge that Khair was in such close proximity to him, was enough to ensure that he made an enormous mess out of the letter he was writing to the Governor General. After innumerable failed attempts and several shredded sheets of the Whatman fine paper he was using, James finally gave up. He needed to clear his head. Pushing his chair back, he briskly rose from it and turned toward the side door that led into the small flower garden outside. As he strode out, he noticed that the late evening shadows had already started playing hide-and-seek between the trees and the parakeets had retired to their nests a while ago. He'd been so busy, he hadn't noticed how late it was. The fountain on the side spouted a steady stream of clear water that made a tinkling sound as it flowed down onto the rocks below, and the evening air was scented with the aroma of a myriad assortment of night-blooming flowers. James closed his eyes. It was one of those moments when time seemed to stand still, almost as if it were waiting with bated breath for something monumental to happen.

'Hello.'

An unknown voice called out, yet it seemed strangely familiar to James, as though he knew it from somewhere. He opened his eyes and slowly turned around. Dusk had settled in by then and it was dark in the garden, but he could see her clearly, silhouetted against the dim light that was coming in from his study. He couldn't make out the colour of her *salwar-kameez*, but James knew that that kind of lustre was only possible with the finest silk. She had a veil wrapped around her head, but she'd allowed it to drop slightly on one side, thus revealing some of her long, dark hair. The face was as beautiful as James remembered from that first sighting, but the eyes that had looked hesitant, almost childlike then, had an oddly purposeful look about them now. Even as she stood there, looking at him, James got the sudden sensation of a hundred secret doors opening from somewhere, leading out into a world that had been unseen before, a world full of possibilities and dreams.

'I overheard someone say that you were in your study.' This time he noticed that her voice had a lilt to it.

'How did you know I was out here?' His voice was so low, it was barely a whisper. There was no one in the garden but the bungalow was full of staff.

'I just knew.'

'You should not be here.' He mechanically took a couple of steps back, but she didn't move from her place.

'My grandfather had to go on campaign,' she said then as though that explained her presence there. 'The Nizam has joined the war with the British.'

James couldn't help smiling. 'I am aware of that,' he said. Then his expression instantly became grim again. 'You should not be here,' he repeated even more firmly this time.

'I could not help it.' Raising her eyes, she then looked at him over her thick, dark eyelashes. There was something so young, so naïve, so innocently irresistible about her, but James's expression gave nothing away as he pursed his lips and shook his head

'You should get back to your mother and grandmother. They must not know that you came here.'

'They already know.' She shrugged and James's eyes widened in surprise. The whole situation seemed unreal, almost surreal to him.

'I told my mother that I am in love with you. She approves.'[48] She lifted her head then, her expression confident, almost defiant.

'Love?' James stared at her. 'What would a young girl like you, know about love?'

'Do not patronise me.' She looked at him indignantly. 'I am just being honest.'

"The Lord detests lying lips but he delights in those who tell the truth." Proverbs 12:22 from the Bible, thought James, and then almost laughed out loud at the absurdity of the situation. Here was the beautiful and determined young woman he'd been thinking about incessantly for days, declaring her unabashed love for him, while all he could do was stand there, quoting lines from the Bible.

'I appreciate your honesty.' Tilting his head slightly, he looked at her out of his clear blue eyes. 'But this is not appropriate.'

'You should admit it too.' She twirled the end of her veil between the thumb and forefinger of her right hand as she looked at him expectantly.

'I am sorry?' James narrowed his eyes then, visibly confused. 'Admit what?'

'That you are in love with me too. I know you are. Go on, admit it.'

He was actually amazed at her confidence. She seemed sure, much too sure of herself. "And, look at me. Almost twice her age and tongue-tied," he reprimanded himself silently.

'This is a precarious situation,' he said to her then. 'Very precarious indeed.'

---

48 Laslocky, Megan. *The Little Book of Heartbreak: Love gone wrong through the ages.* USA. Plume, a member of Penguin Group, USA. January, 2013.

Precarious or not, James had to confess to himself that there really was something deliriously tempting about the scenario playing out in front of him. The lady standing merely a few steps away, the silence of the night and the heady scent of the garden abounding with night-blooming blossoms. The iridescent, white moonflowers with their heart-shaped leaves and prickly stems were among his favourites. They always uncurled themselves after sunset, giving off a mesmerising fragrance all night, but strangely, they seemed to emanate an almost heavenly aroma tonight.

Or was it her? His curiosity now aroused; James took one tentative step forward.

And then, as though that was all she needed, Khair quickly crossed the short distance between them and walked straight into his arms. James, too shocked at the boldness of her move and too horrified at what might happen if anyone saw them, didn't react at all at first. He simply stayed there, as though rooted to the spot even as her body pressed into his, willing him to understand the urgency of her desire. The veil that had covered her head had fallen off and was now lying discarded on the ground, and her dark hair was splayed all over his shoulders as she wrapped her arms around him. Even as her delicate hands moved rhythmically along the length of his back, James just stood motionless, still, repeating over and over to himself that this wasn't real, wasn't really happening. Perhaps all the thinking and wondering and fantasizing had really made him lose his mind. But it went on until he finally realized that it wasn't his imagination or even a dream, gathered that this was really happening, that she really was in his arms, here between the moonflower beds and the tinkling water fountain, beyond and past any semblance of rational thought. Surely, any man would have given in to a desire that was so natural, a desire that he'd been desperately trying to quell ever since the first time that he'd laid eyes on this beautiful young woman.

Inhaling deeply, James removed his right hand from the pocket of his breeches. Placing it under her chin, he lifted her face ever so slightly. The beautiful kohled eyes were half-closed, a faraway expression on her lovely face. The tiny beauty mark above her chin was tantalizingly near and he could distinctly hear every intake of her breath. Encircling her waist with his other arm, he drew her even closer. She raised her face toward him, the rosebud lips trembling. Even as he bent his head to kiss her, it seemed to James as though there was a tiny voice somewhere in his head, a voice that was urgently trying to tell him something. James didn't want to know anything anymore. His mind had stopped working. Thinking, considering, deliberating – it was far too late for all that now.

'Eeeee....eeeee.....eeeeee!'

They both jumped at the sudden screeching and Khair's eyes snapped open. The alarm on her face was palpable as they frantically looked around to see where the sound had come from. Just then, a parakeet with a bright blue crest and yellow beak came flying out, seemingly from nowhere. There was a sudden gust of wind as it flew past, right above their heads, and then as quickly as it had appeared, it seemed to vanish somewhere between the tall mango trees on the other side of the garden. Khair, who was still too astounded to react, simply stood there, staring after the disappearing bird, a bemused expression on her face. As for James, the sudden intrusion had been more than enough to break the spell and jolt him back to reality. Coming to his senses, he shook his head, placed both hands on her shoulders and as gently as he could, pushed her away from him. His heart was still beating as frantically as before, but at least his mind seemed to be in a more rational place. And then, before she could object or even react to his refusal, he thrust his hands into the pockets of his breeches, turned around and walked away. Away from the enchanting lady who still stood there, waiting, watching, perhaps in the hope that he might change his mind. Admittedly, it did take all his willpower to walk away from her, but even as he crossed the few steps across the garden and opened the door that led into his study, he couldn't help thinking that the mesmerising fragrance that had taken over his senses that night, hadn't been the moonflowers. It had most certainly, been her.

6
Love and War

If Lord Wellesley had seemed aggressive and ambitious before, these days he was like a man obsessed. The war with Tipu was on, the pressure was palpable and the political atmosphere naturally distrustful. Considering that this was the fourth Anglo Mysore war, more than six years after the third one when Lord Cornwallis had scrapped the Sultan's name from the list of the Company's "friends", it was but natural that the desperation to win was at a frenzied level. The third Anglo-Mysore war had resulted in a defeat for Tipu, but the British had failed to seize his capital city of Seringapatam.[49] This time the objective was clear and it was the Governor General's own brother who was leading this fourth war. Not surprisingly, Arthur Wellesley who was much like his older brother as far as his approach toward India was concerned, was proving to be a determined and grim adversary for the Sultan, hell-bent on winning at any cost.

After the defeat and humiliation that he'd suffered during the third Anglo Mysore war, Tipu had focused his entire attention on strengthening his military prowess with help from Arabia, Turkey, Afghanistan, and of course, the French. Tipu's ardent admiration for the ideologies of the French Revolution was no secret since he'd

49 Campbell, Ryan. La Salle University. *The Histories. Richard Wellesley and the Fourth Anglo Mysore War.* Volume 15, Issue 1. 2019.

been candidly expressing this in letters to the French government. He had in fact, as a gesture of solidarity to the Jacobin Club, also planted a Tree of Liberty in Seringapatam around 1794. The British though, were another matter. If the Sultan was outspoken about his appreciation for the French, then he was equally honest about how much he detested the British. There was certainly no love lost there. The feelings of animosity were of course mutual, and in fact, the involvement of the French made things even more complicated. The Governor General tended to take anything associated with the French more personally and this made his resolve that much stronger to destroy the state of Mysore, once and for all.[50] And, after the Subsidiary Alliance, and with the Nizam having disbanded his French forces, it was clear to everyone where the loyalties of the Hyderabad durbar were, as far as this war was concerned.[51]

March and April usually marked the onset of Spring in India, but in several places, it could feel more like a straight leap into summer. April was always a hot month in Hyderabad, with soaring daily temperatures. But that year with the war, the heat was on in more ways than one. Despite the British being in the superior position, Tipu had never been an enemy to be taken lightly. Added to that was the fact that he had recently fortified his capital, and increased the number of his infantry and cavalry. Of course, the British attack being commanded by Major General David Baird only made the situation that much more tense. After all, Baird was the Sultan's sworn enemy after he had been held in captivity by Tipu's

50 Chancey, Marla Karen. In the Company's Secret Service. Thesis. Florida State University Library. 2003.

51 Campbell, Ryan. La Salle University. *The Histories. Richard Wellesley and the Fourth Anglo Mysore War.* Volume 15, Issue 1. 2019.

father, Hyder Ali, following the disastrous British defeat in the 1780 Battle of Pollilur.[52]

As expected, the fighting was intense and went on incessantly for several weeks. On the night of 3 May however, a decision was taken and around midday the next day, the final attack by the British was launched on the fort. One of the Sultan's most loyal *sipahsalars*, Sayyid Abdul Ghaffar, was killed by a cannon ball. Then, protected with covering fire from British batteries, the attackers crossed the four-foot-deep Cauvery River, defeated the defenders within minutes and stormed the fort. The rest of the attack was also short, swift and brutal, lasting all of a few hours. The fort was taken and then the Sultan shot dead. He died after having suffered three bayonet wounds as well as a head shot. Dressed in all his finery, he had lived up to his name and had fought like a tiger until the very end, shooting his enemies one after another, his attendants handing him musket after musket.[53] In the end, he died like a soldier, refusing to settle for peace on humiliating terms. It was a sure victory for the Britishers though, a win so great that when General Harris, the Commander of the English Army, heard about the Sultan's death, he triumphantly exclaimed, 'Today India is ours!' Tipu Sultan, the most-feared Eastern King, "the tyrant" was finally dead![54]

However, it didn't end there. After the death of the Sultan, the siege that followed was one of the most violent, most vicious ones

---

52 https://en.wikipedia.org/wiki/Battle_of_Pollilur_(1780)

53 Giddings, Robert. *Imperial Echoes: Eye Witness Accounts of Victoria's Little Wars.* Great Britain. Leo Cooper. An Imprint of Pen & Sword Books Ltd. Great Britain. 1996.

54 Brittlebank, Kate. Seven things you might have not known about Tipu Sultan, India's first freedom fighter. Scroll. Excerpted with permission from *Tiger: The Life of Tipu Sultan*, Kate Brittlebank, Juggernaut. 22 July 2016.

that had ever been witnessed. The Sultan's beloved island city that had been lovingly built by his father Hyder Ali, and rightly described as "the richest, most convenient, and beautiful spot possessed in the present age by any native prince in India" by the British Military Commander, Captain Alexander Dirom in the year 1792, was reduced to a hotbed of violent crime within hours. The mighty fort, rich industrial suburbs of Ganjam and Lalbagh and glorious pleasure gardens became a thing of the past as the bloodshed, rapine and looting continued, unabated. Jewels, bars of gold, even the ornately carved doors of the palace and Tipu's own clothing were sold in the camp bazaars. In fact, such was the extent of the destruction that it seemed to those who witnessed it, as though not a single house had been spared.[55]

For James, the weeks that followed this victory were the kind that can take an unimaginable toll on anyone, particularly a well-intentioned, honourable man. The manner in which the divisions of the spoils of the war took place was the primary reason for the deep rifts that eventually occurred between the Britishers and the Nizam. James, who had worked very hard to solidify this relationship, found it distressing to the extent that the situation had a detrimental impact on his health and state-of-mind. Promises were blatantly broken, commitments were forgotten and loyalties that should have been regarded were instead, treated with the utmost negligence. The Nizam, who should have been rewarded generously, was cast aside and the ancient Wadyar dynasty was given huge chunks of the spoils. This was a deal agreed by Mir Alam who, though popular with the Britishers, was no longer considered

55 Kumar, Krishna R. When the sun set on Seringapatam. *The Hindu.* 4 May 2017.

trustworthy by the Nizam. Naturally, the Nizam felt that since he had contributed a significant part of the army for the war, he should have received a more substantial part of the spoils and this went on to become a major point of contention.[56] It was therefore evident that the aftermath of the war had resulted in creating a general feeling of mistrust and suspicion in the city. To add to that, James was finding it increasingly difficult to conceal his true feelings as far as the Governor General was concerned. They had never really been on the same page, but these days, James found himself inwardly recoiling at some of the blatantly dishonourable strategies being adopted by his superior in Calcutta.

Life is frequently bittersweet, and those days undoubtedly had that quality. Between all the tension and stress that was increasingly becoming a part of his official life, there was the magic of the affair that had started between Khair-un-Nissa and him. Of course, the affair itself was bittersweet in many ways, after all, it wasn't an easy situation for either of them. Constantly aware of the perils of the relationship, James had tried, several times in fact, to resist, to refrain, abstain. After that first meeting in the garden, he'd tried to convince himself that they'd both just been swept up in the moment, that it wouldn't happen again. He'd also been inwardly thankful that he'd managed to resist her charms, even secretly thanking that parakeet for making an appearance at the right moment and snapping him out of the trance that he'd obviously been in.

Khair-un-Nissa though, was a much more insistent young woman than James had realized. Convinced that she had fallen deeply in love with him, she managed to slip into the Residency and

56 Nanisetti, Sarish. Mir Alam Bahadur is remembered for his gifts to Hyderabad. *The Hindu*. March 30th, 2019.

make her way to James's bedroom one evening. To say that James was astounded when he saw her there would be an understatement, but the fact that she claimed to have the support of her mother and grandmother should not have been as shocking as it was to him. After all, a mother is a mother. How could she not have prioritized the happiness of her daughter, particularly a free-thinking and rational woman like Sharaf-un-Nissa? As for James, despite his reservations, he was a human being in the end and when have mere human beings been able to resist the irresistible? Particularly when a girl as lovely as her, repeatedly claimed her love for him, swearing that she would rather die than be apart? It was astonishing of course that a girl who could otherwise seem as reticent as Khair-un-Nissa, could be so openly vocal about her feelings. Repeated mention of the inaptness of the relationship and the disgrace and pain it would inevitably bring, brought on a strange sort of stubbornness in her, almost as though she was deliberately closing her eyes to something that was as stark as the day. Reminders of the fact that she was already engaged to someone else brought on tears, rage and ultimately threats to end her life. James was also painfully aware of the fact that she was more honest than him, since she was fearlessly voicing the thoughts that he himself had, but didn't have the courage to say out loud. Of course, that didn't deter Khair. She kept at it until finally, her persistence paid off and James's resolve broke. Blocking his mind to everything else, he banished all rational thought, abandoned all misgivings, and finally gave in to the desperate calling of his heart and body.

The days they spent together after that, wrapped in each other's arms, oblivious to all but each other, had an incredible, almost illusory feeling about them. Then again, it sometimes seemed to

James that those moments with Khair were the only ones that were real, everything else was an impression. Afterward, they would lie in his four-poster bed, watching the sun from the bedroom window as it started descending the city's skyline, down into the blue waters of the Musi. Sometimes it felt to the two lovers as though the river itself was giving them her blessing. But then, this wasn't the first time she had witnessed the union of two people who loved each other. Way back in the sixteenth century, before he became ruler of Golconda, Muhammad Quli Qutab Shah used to cross the river to meet his beloved, a local dancer by the name of Bhagmati who lived in a tiny hut in the village of Chichlam, on the southern bank of the river. According to a legend, it was the tinkling of her anklets and the melodious voice in which she sang that made the young prince fall in love with her. In fact, so besotted was he with the beautiful dancer, that he would cross the river in spite of the raging floods that often engulfed it, to meet her. His father, who didn't want his son risking his life, built a bridge over the river to make it easy for his son to cross it. Then, when they got married, Quli Qutab Shah who was emperor by then, built a new city where Chichlam once stood. He named the city Bhagnagar, thereafter even shifting the capital there.[57] Eventually, when Bhagmati converted to Islam, taking the name of Hyder Mahal, the emperor renamed the city Hyderabad to honour his wife.[58] And that was how the city of Hyderabad got its name.

The city of Hyderabad was no stranger to love. Of course, love is usually not simple, it wasn't then and it couldn't be now either. James and Khair were as aware of the adversities that would undoubtedly

57 Interview and tour with Mr. S Anand, Registered Guide, Dept of Tourism, Govt of Telangana. January, 2022.

58 Interview with Salma Yusuf Hussain. Food Historian and Persian Scholar. May, 2022.

be strewn in their path as they were sure of their feelings for each other. Of course, neither of them, not even Khair, was naïve enough to assume that others would ever completely be able to understand the relationship that had changed the course of their lives. In fact, James knew that despite condemning it, on some level, most of the people would comprehend the desperation with which Khair and he were physically drawn to each other. What would have seemed astonishing to them, however, was the effortlessness with which they connected, communicated. After all, how could two people who came from completely different worlds, share such a deep understanding with each other? It seemed so inconceivable; it was perhaps just easier for people to accept that the physical aspect of their relationship was the only one that existed. Yet James knew that beyond the frantic love making, beyond any carnal desire, above any basic physical need, he had really started to care about Khair. Her honesty, her vulnerability, her oblivion, the strength and fortitude that he now knew she was capable of, it all came together and made it nearly impossible for him to detach himself emotionally. Attraction was one thing, love was another, but the burning need to take care of her, to protect and honour her, that was what worried him the most.

And so, it went on that way. The air of the city though overwhelmingly heavy with the strain of treachery and betrayal, was also at the same time, redolent with the fragrance of a love that was blossoming and blooming with each passing day. It was almost as though the soul of the love story that had given the city its name was still alive in the aura that surrounded it, bestowing a blessing on all those who dared to live for love.

7
Falling Leaves

Autumn, the golden season! A time for new beginnings. It was on one such glorious autumn evening that year, that James was sitting in his study and happened to glance out of the window. From his vantage point at the desk, James had an excellent view of the garden and he couldn't help smiling as he looked at it now. The trees outside were changing colour, those warm hues that always seemed to radiate a splendour that could only be seen at this time of the year. Before long, the leaves would start falling and the garden would be strewn with them, a magnificent patchwork carpet of reds and browns. Soon, all the leaves would have fallen and blown away, and then the trees would start readying themselves for rebirth. Rebirth! There was so much promise in that word. As though the season itself embodied the faith that life could and would start all over again. Well, hope and faith really did seem to be the only things that he could cling to as well. Hope and faith that somehow, someway, the relationship between him and Khair-un-Nissa would manage to stand the tests that it was going to undoubtedly be subjected to.

Turning back to his desk, he re-read the letter that had come in from his half-brother William. Despite the regular exchange of correspondence between them, James hadn't yet confessed the truth about Khair to his brother. The ten-year age difference between

William and him notwithstanding, the two of them had always been close.

They usually discussed all matters with ease, but the affair with Khair was far too delicate a subject. Of course, James was well aware of what William's reaction to an admission like this would have been. At the very least, he couldn't imagine William being at all pleased about the very difficult choices that James had made.[59] His brother would never understand how he had been rendered utterly helpless in the face of a pull so compelling. How could he tell him about that first time when she had approached him, declared her passionate love[60] and everything that had happened thereafter? How could he admit the fact that an already challenging situation had been made even more difficult by the sheer beauty she possessed? Only James himself knew that despite being well aware of the perils of the situation, it had been impossible to hold himself back. He could never have explained to another human being how he had truly tried his hardest to resist. Nor could he admit to anyone how exhausting it was to sway between the extreme feelings that he was experiencing these days. The ecstasy of being with her, the stress of what would happen in the future, the guilt he felt about the pain it was causing to people like Baqar. Baqar! James shook his head as his thoughts turned to the old man.

He'd been a good friend to James, he'd always regarded him as a trusted brother, the last thing James wanted to do was to cause him so much anguish. James knew that if news about the affair got out, it

---

59 Laslocky, Megan. *The Little Book of Heartbreak: Love gone wrong through the ages.* USA. Plume, a member of Penguin Group, USA. January, 2013.

60 Carlyle and "Irving's London Circle": *Some Unpublished Letters by Thomas Carlyle and Mrs. Edward Strachey.* Vol 69, No. 5 pp 1135-1149. J. Calder, Grace. Cambridge University Press. Dec 1954.

would undoubtedly bring terrible shame and dishonour to his former friend's family. It was a precarious situation. Too many people were likely to get hurt, even destroyed. But what could he do? If there was anything that could reduce a man to complete helplessness, then it most certainly was love. And he was in love with Khair-un-Nissa.

With a sigh, he settled down to write out a response to William. He was just finishing when his *munshi* came to see him. James quickly scrawled his name at the bottom of the letter and covered the sheets with a heavy paperweight. He then smiled up at the older man, who was still standing by the door, waiting to be called in.

'Come in Aziz. How is everything?' James was fond of his munshi, a loyal and very intelligent man.[61] In that sense, James considered himself lucky. He had a wonderful assistant in Henry Russell,[62] and an equally dedicated and efficient munshi in Aziz Ullah.

'Everything is fine Sahib.' Aziz took one of the chairs on the other side of the desk. 'Would you be attending the celebration party tonight at Masarrat Mahal?'

James nodded. 'Yes, I will be going. Also, I intend to visit the durbar tomorrow. Perhaps I should take a nice present?'

James knew that the situation with Khair wasn't the only matter of concern for him these days. The warm and close relationship that he'd shared with the Nizam's durbar had come under tremendous strain after the fall of Seringapatam. Of course, despite feeling hurt and betrayed about the shabby way in which he had been treated after the war, the Nizam was on a personal level, very fond of James.

61 Wilkinson, Callie. *Relationships between the Political Residents of the English East India Company and their munshis, 1798-1818.* Wolfson College, University of Cambridge.

62 The Russells of Swallowfield Park. Swallowfield Park Case Study, UK. East India Company at Home, 1757-1857.

It was a feeling that James reciprocated and he knew that he had to concentrate on recovering his previous friendship with the durbar. It was where he drew his strength from and what made him such a successful diplomat and so precious to the Company as well.

'It was not your fault Sahib,' remarked Aziz Ullah then, as though reading James's thoughts. 'You did what you had to. I am sure everyone knows that inwardly; you do not agree with the Governor General on these matters.'

James smiled wryly at the munshi's words. The camaraderie between the Governor General and William had been instant when they'd first met at the Cape. In fact, William had made quite an impression on Wellesley, so much so, that the Governor General had even offered him the position of Confidential Military Secretary, and brought him back to Calcutta with him.[63] Despite being fond of his brother, however, the Governor General had never taken the same liking toward James.

'Never mind that,' said James then, turning his attention back to Aziz. 'What shall we take as a present when we visit the durbar tomorrow? A pair of pigeons? He is a keen connoisseur, after all.'[64]

'Yes, he is certainly fond of his pigeons.' The older man smiled. He knew James was talking about the Nizam. 'That would make a fine present indeed. And perhaps you should give a *nazar*[65] too? He has not been looking too well, of late.'

---

63 Kirkpatrick, William (1754-1812). *Dictionary of National Biography*, 1885-1900. U.K.

64 Wilkinson, Callie Hannah. Dissertation on "The Residents of the British East India Company at Indian Royal Courts" c. 1798-1818. Wolfson College. University of Cambridge. July, 2017.

65 A nazar is an eye-shaped amulet believed to protect against the evil eye according to multiple traditions.

James stroked his chin thoughtfully. The Nizam had seemed frailer recently, which was worrisome. He had been a sturdy and robust man in his youth, but age certainly seemed to be catching up with him now.

'A nazar is a good idea.' James nodded his agreement. 'That is settled then. Was there anything else?'

'Nothing of any major importance. What time will you be leaving for the party tonight?'

'7:30. Could you ask my valet to make sure the palanquin is ready?'

'Very good, Sahib.' Aziz Ullah rose from his seat, bowed slightly to James and then quietly left the room. Glancing at his pocket watch, James realized that he was now running late for the party. He picked up the letter he had written to William, slipped it into an envelope and sealed it with sealing wax, ready to be sent in the next day's daak. Then he hurriedly pushed back his chair and got up. Despite the beautiful weather outside, it had been a nerve-wracking evening. All that thinking and contemplating had exhausted him and it would be good to relax in the bath before he started getting ready for the party.

As usual, the party at Masarrat Mahal was a grand affair. That of course wasn't surprising since despite the general air of tension in the city, the victory against the Sultan had been too momentous a feat to simply be ignored and the celebrations had been on in full swing with ghazals and dance performances going on day after day. With the weather turning cooler and the air crisper, the gardens of the palaces were the obvious choice for the parties these days. Decked up with fairy lights and shamiana tents, the gardens looked ethereal and the perfumed night air resonated with soulful *sarangi*, *tabla* and *manjeera* music, intermittently punctuated with the luxurious rustle of the finest silk. The dance girls who performed at these affairs were always the best in the city and the *mor ka naach*, *patang naach* and *qahar ka naach* were the more popular forms of dance. The musicians were also the most celebrated ones. Syrah flowed copiously and the dinner that followed was never less than a magnificent feast, fit for several kings. It was no wonder then, that the parties were always well-attended and like everyone else, James too enjoyed himself immensely and was, in fact, often there until the very end.

Much like the season itself, it seemed as though there was something in the air of the city during those days that was heralding in a time of transition, as if change and transformation were now inevitable. In fact, even while the celebration parties were on, the dynamics among the highest thrones of command in Hyderabad were swiftly changing. So much so, that to say that interpersonal relations were strained, would be an understatement. Pure hatred, loathing and even the desire to resort to any means to witness the downfall of one's foe, were the general feelings among those who had previously been congenial and to a great extent, even friendly toward each other. And even though there was an overall feeling of hostility in the air, there was one person who seemed to be at the receiving end of almost everyone's wrath. Mir Alam, the Prime Minister's Private Secretary, had offended a lot of people, including the Prime Minister and even the Nizam. There had been something cocky, sly and underhand about his behaviour during the war, and rumours were rife that he had secretly hoarded away huge wealth after the siege of Seringapatam.[66] Yes, he had done well for himself and was even in the good books of the Britishers, but his attitude and disloyalty toward his own people hadn't gone unnoticed. And though there was no immediate action taken against him, it was almost as if a silent fire had slowly started simmering. If he had paid attention to the animosity that he had evoked around himself, Mir Alam would have known that sooner or later, the inferno was inevitable.

---

66 Nanisetti, Sarish. Mir Alam Bahadur is remembered for his gifts to Hyderabad. The Hindu. March 30th, 2019.

8
No Retreat, No Surrender

People had started talking. First, it had been furtive, the kind of stealthy exchanges that involve hushed whispers and pursed lips behind the veneer of other things. Then all of a sudden, it became blatantly deliberate, almost as though the secret was brazen, too brazen to deserve to be protected by the charade of pretence.

Khair of course, was much in love to be perturbed by a bit of malicious gossip. James was wiser to the ways of the world and when a particularly vicious piece appeared in a local newspaper one day, he knew that it had gone too far.[67]

'I cannot trouble myself with a useless piece of gossip that nobody will even bother reading.' Khair tried to appear nonchalant but James knew that she was acting all brave. After all, even she couldn't deny the inevitable scandal that this would cause.

'It is not a nice piece,' James said then with a worried frown. 'It...'

'I am not interested in the article. I am only interested in the truth.' There was a stubborn look on her face, the pink rosebud lips pressed together firmly. As though closing her eyes to something would make it go away. How comforting naivete could be!

67 Dadabhoy, Bakhtiar K. *The Magnificent Diwan: The Life and Times of Sir Salar Jung 1*. India. Penguin Random House. 13 December 2019.

'And what is the truth, my darling?' James asked her, raising his eyebrows enquiringly.

'The truth is that I love you and cannot live without you!'

'Is youth always so dramatic?' James laughed, his blue eyes twinkling. Then almost instantly, his expression changed. 'You should take it seriously. After all, you are engaged to someone else and...'

'Mention him once more and I promise you, I shall end my life!'

Closing his eyes briefly, James sighed. She couldn't keep using that as a threat, as a means to procrastinate, put off discussing a matter of such great importance. 'You really cannot talk your way out with threats every time I try to have a sensible conversation with you. This is a grave issue. Bazaar gossip is not a simple thing. It has serious political repercussions.[68] Baqar...'

'This is all his fault!' Khair instantly looked enraged at the mention of her grandfather. 'He has been behaving like a victim ever since he returned to Hyderabad. He never should have interfered in my life, fixing my marriage with that adolescent!' If the situation hadn't been as grave as James knew it was, he might even have been amused at how much Khair loathed her fiancé. She could hardly bear the mere mention of his name.

'He has his own problems,' James said then, referring to Baqar-Ali-Khan. He knew the older man hadn't had an easy time with people from his community gossiping and talking about him. 'If anything, we need to be careful of the others.'

That was true. The atmosphere in the city was anything but easy. In any case, certainly not easy enough to take kindly to an affair between a young girl belonging to the ruling family and a

68 Interview with Dr Shankar Kumar, Noted Historian, Hindu College, Delhi University. Dec, 2021.

much older British diplomat. The tension between Aristu Jah and Mir Alam, and the durbar and the British was palpable these days. It seemed as though either of them would do anything to disgrace the other. If Mir Alam was sly, then Aristu Jah was equally shrewd. If the Nizam was discontented and disillusioned with the British, then the Company had made its displeasure clear as well. Between all of that, James couldn't help but wonder. Where exactly did Khair and he stand? After all, he'd worked with all of them long enough to know one thing very well. When it came to the crux of honour, control and personal scores, then it was human nature to resort to any means to get what they wanted.

'We need to be careful,' he said again as she watched him and then frowned.

'What does that mean? I cannot stop meeting you, that is certain. I am willing to do anything else.'

James shook his head. He wasn't suggesting that they stop meeting. How could he? He loved her too much.

'I cannot even fathom giving you up,' she repeated then, even more firmly. 'I am telling you; I would much rather die!'

Wrapping his arm around her, he drew her close. From his four-poster bed, they could see the tops of the tallest trees in the gardens below, swaying gently in the breeze. It was a cold winter afternoon, but the sun had come out and with its dappled rays falling on the trees, some of the older leaves looked like burnished gold. 'Just like the colour of your hair,' she teased him then, as they looked out of the window together. She took a strand of his curly hair between her thumb and index finger and twirled it around playfully. 'You worry too much, *Eshgham*[69],' she said, using her special endearment for him.

69 'My Love' in Persian, this word is used to call loved ones in Iran.

It was what she called him when they were alone. Now, turning over to face him, she propped herself up on her elbow, her chin resting in the palm of her hand. 'Have you not heard the saying? "If the house of the world is dark, Love will find a way to create windows," said Jalal ad-Din Mohammad Rumi. The famous Persian poet, scholar and Sufi mystic, in case you did not know.'

'I know, my darling, I know.' He smiled at her. There was something so young and hopeful about her, he wanted to believe it too. Perhaps he really was overthinking. With a sigh, he gathered her in his arms again.

As it turned out, he was wrong about that. For not long after the newspaper article had appeared, a furious Mir Alam, who had recently firmly established himself in the good books of the Company, wrote directly to Lord Wellesley to investigate the rumoured affair between James Achilles Kirkpatrick and Khair-un-Nissa. He alleged that the Resident who had been appointed there to ensure harmony and cordial relations between the British and the Hyderabadis, was doing just the opposite. He further lamented that James had angered the local community by bringing disgrace to the ruling family and needed to be taught a lesson. He then urged the Governor General to investigate the affair thoroughly and severely punish the Resident, if he was found guilty of the allegations. At a time when the Britishers were trying to consolidate their power in India, this kind of controversy was the last thing they needed.[70] And so, an official investigation against James Achilles Kirkpatrick was approved and launched.[71]

---

70 Interview with Dr. Shankar Kumar, Noted Historian, Hindu College, Delhi University. Dec, 2021.

71 Laslocky, Megan. *The Little Book of Heartbreak: Love gone wrong through the ages.* USA. Plume, a member of Penguin Group, USA. January, 2013.

James knew that as an employee of the Company, he was completely and unconditionally answerable to his superiors in Calcutta. He was also aware that with changing attitudes and increased prejudices, things had become more stringent. Of course, it hadn't always been like that, in fact, there had been a time when it was hardly uncommon for a British officer to live with or marry a local Hindu or Muslim lady. Even Calcutta, the capital of British India, had a substantial Anglo-Indian community. That was in the free and easy days of the Company, but now, intermingling was frowned upon and looked at with suspicion.[72] In fact, James had even heard that the Wellesley brothers had been especially despatched to India to put an end to this easy mixing. It wouldn't be surprising then, that with Wellesley personally involved, this investigation against him was going to be extremely thorough. His colleagues would be questioned and cross-examined. Nothing would be left out, nothing spared. Even his sexual life would be subjected to rigorous and humiliating examination. It was no longer a private matter between Khair and him; it was now a question of his loyalty to his government. And of course, the impact that a scandal of this sort would have on the relations between the Company and the Hyderabadis, could not be overstated. Considering the enormity of the situation, James knew that when the truth about his affair came out, he would have to pay the price. And it would undoubtedly be a heavy price. Bracing himself, James started mentally preparing for what would most certainly be a very harrowing time indeed.

Of course, any investigation in the city had to be routed via the Nizam and his Prime Minister. This proved to be lucky for James since Aristu Jah had always been fond of him. Naturally though,

72 Interview with Rana Safvi. Historian and Writer. May, 2022.

mere fondness was not the only reason for the approach that the Prime Minister took. It was common knowledge that there was no love lost between Aristu Jah and Mir Alam. In fact, their animosity had never been as blatant as it was these days. A shrewd and sharp politician, Aristu knew an opportunity as soon as he spotted one and he instantly saw the investigation against James as a wonderful chance to teach Mir Alam the lesson of his life.[73]

And so, unbeknownst to anyone else, he invited James to his palace one day for the sport of cockfighting. This was nothing new, since the two of them often got together for their favourite sport. Well aware of how fond the Prime Minister was of this particular sport, James had on several occasions managed to source quality cocks from England for his friend. He knew Aristu Jah had a particular liking for the red pyles, he thought they were the true game cocks, particularly the exact five pounders. 'You will never see a red pyle break away,' Aristu always said confidently. 'They are the real fighters, the scarlet ones.' He kept their tails, manes and nails nicely clipped, spurs always sharp and strong, made sure they were given a nutritious diet of oats, wheat and barley and was able to instantly recognize the ones with the "no retreat, no surrender" mentality.

The first fight of the day was between a red pyle and a blue-black and lasted only eleven minutes, but it was a good one. There was a rain of feathers and both birds were badly wounded by then, but the red pyle wasn't ready to give up. 'No retreat, no surrender,' remarked Aristu Jah as they both watched, eyes riveted on the pit. 'Just like I always say.'

---

73 Dadabhoy, Bakhtiar K. *The Magnificent Diwan: The Life and Times of Sir Salar Jung 1.* India. Penguin Random House. 13 December 2019.

'Perhaps it was squeezed,' said James with a sly look at the Prime Minister. 'That would be a foul.'

'You never need to squeeze a red pyle,' retorted Aristu Jah without batting an eyelid. 'Never.'

As predicted, the red pyle won and the fight ended with the blue-black dead. The second fight was even shorter, lasting all of seven minutes, but by the time the third fight started between a black and a red pyle, James had understood that there was more on the Prime Minister's mind than just the game. James knew Aristu Jah quite well and by then, he had gauged that this wasn't simply a social engagement. And even though, like always, James did accompany him into the palace after the fight, it was clear that the easy banter and exchange of political gossip that usually followed after the cockfighting was not on the agenda today. Instead, after a single round of Syrah and hookah, Aristu Jah came straight to the point, candidly apprising James of the investigation that had been opened against him in Calcutta.

'Of course, there are ways to get out of this if we work together,' he added in the end. 'If you cooperate with me, you will be out of this situation quickly and...' Aristu paused for effect and bent in closer. The thick drapes at the windows had been tightly drawn and the room was too dark for James to make out the expression on his face. The glint in his hawk-like eyes was clear enough though. 'You can even keep the girl.'

He then leaned back into the soft contours of the divan he was sitting in, assuming a more relaxed position. His dark eyes however were still firmly fixed on James as he put his pipe back into his mouth. White aromatic fumes rose up from the wooden pipe, forming misty, elusive rings around them. No sooner had they encircled the air and disappeared, that the new ones arose.

'Mir Alam has been getting much too big for his boots lately. He needs to be got rid of.' The Prime Minister's voice was clear and confident. 'Fire him from the position of the Company's *vakil.* Once he is fired, he will no longer be in charge of the newly conquered territories. I will then convince the Nizam to clear your name of all this.[74] Mir Alam will likely be thrown into the dungeons and that will be the end of his power. You can then...er...carry on as before.'

James knew he meant the affair with Khair. He also knew that even though Aristu was laying it out as a friendly offer, the Prime Minister was well aware that James didn't have a lot of choices.

'It would be a winning situation for both of us, Hushmat Jung. You know that.'

James did know that. He closed his eyes for a brief moment, trying to fathom the consequences of his decision. He never had liked Mir Alam. Too sly, even underhand at times. And he was desperate to solidify his relationship with the Nizam. Not to forget that this might well be the best for Hyderabad. If Mir Alam was dismissed as the Company's vakil, Aristu Jah would most certainly take his place. And...

'She is a lovely girl, that one.' Aristu's voice interrupted his thoughts. 'And would indeed be miserable if they marry her off to that boy. I hear she finds him quite loathsome.' He shrugged and straightened the string of pearls around his neck. 'Just in case you require more convincing.'

James didn't. His mind instantly made up, he nodded at the Prime Minister who then came forward to embrace him warmly. 'You know how fond I am of you, Hushmat Jung. As is the Nizam.

---

74 Dadabhoy, Bakhtiar K. *The Magnificent Diwan: The Life and Times of Sir Salar Jung 1.* India. Penguin Random House. 13 December 2019.

You are one of us, after all.' He patted the younger man on the back. 'I like winners. That goes for cock fighting and other things as well.'

Smiling broadly, Aristu Jah then steered James towards the enormous carved door at the entrance of the palace. 'And now this is settled, how about another round? Red against red this time.'

9
The Calm

With Mir Alam gone and James back in the Nizam's good graces, things seemed to settle down. Life in Hyderabad was peaceful once again. The investigation had been dropped, all was well between the two lovers and Aristu Jah was delighted with James. The Prime Minister was elated with the way Mir Alam had been disgraced, punished and banished from the city. As far as he was concerned, Mir Alam deserved every bit of it. James, however, had known politicians long enough to understand that if and when push came to shove, they would do anything and everything to reclaim their previous power. Mir Alam was no exception to the rule. In fact, a brutally ambitious man like him would never be able to accept the kind of downfall and humiliation he had suffered. And of course, his imprisonment after the dismissal had only resulted in adding insult to injury. Every time he thought about it, James found himself growing restless and agitated, a feeling akin to that of waiting quietly for a storm that you know is sure to arrive, sooner or later.

He spoke to Khair about it one evening when they were strolling languidly side-by-side in the garden outside his study. She was looking particularly lovely that evening and as she stopped and bent down to inhale the fragrance of the tiny white moonflowers in their beds, James was suddenly overcome with desire for her. Coincidentally, they were at that moment standing in the exact spot where she had approached him for the very first time and James suddenly wished he could take her to his bedroom right then. It was strange actually, given the fact that they'd already made love twice that evening, but James wasn't surprised. He'd had many women in his life, both European as well as Indian, but none of them had been able to ignite the kind of feelings he felt for this one. Sometimes he still couldn't believe that this was really happening, this...this crazy, incredible thing that had started between them. Then of course, who knew how and where it would go. Trying not to think about all that, he turned his mind back to Mir Alam.

'He will not just go away, you know.' He looked at Khair as she rose from the flower bed. 'We cannot simply wish him away.'

'No, he will turn up like a bad penny when he is least wanted,' she laughed, knowing who he was talking about and he couldn't help but wonder how she always managed to comprehend everything he said. There was an inexplicable understanding between them.

'He knows people in the Company,' said James. 'They like him.'

'Well, it did not do him any good the last time.' Khair shrugged, but then her expression became serious. 'My grandfather has been restless as well lately. Do not forget he is popular in the Company too.'

James smiled. Despite her age and naivete, Khair was an intelligent and perceptive young woman. In that sense, she was much like her mother. But then, her astute understanding of politics was hardly surprising since it was common for women like Khair-un-Nissa to take an active interest in these things. Even the Nizam often depended on his two oldest wives for advice about matters of policy. Moreover, anyone who assumed that the affairs of the state were being run solely by the men, was mistaken. The world behind the veils and the curtains was a powerful one, one that could heavily influence, sway and manipulate the one outside.[75] In the earlier days, it used to be the older matriarchs like mothers and aunts and then in Akbar's reign, it was the foster mothers and wet nurses who started playing an active role in the affairs. Like Maham Anga, thought James as he remembered the story he had heard about Akbar's chief nurse and how she was known to have had enormous influence on him. She had almost ruled through him, so much so, that it had even come to be known as the "petticoat government". Yes, some of the women had been so powerful that they had even been called "king makers".[76] But why only that? After all, Razia Sultana had herself been a great monarch. She'd even discarded the veil, appearing in court in male dress and had gone on to rule Delhi for four years. What a glorious period it had been for Delhi!

'Tough women they were,' said James then. 'Traveling while pregnant, delivering babies on the move, joining their menfolk in battle.'

'What are you talking about?' Khair looked confused and James laughed.

'Never mind. I was just thinking out loud.'

He suddenly pressed a finger to his temple and grimaced. The headaches seemed to have become more frequent these days.

'Are you all right, Eshgham?' Khair was beside him at once, concern etched on her beautiful face. 'You seem to be in pain.'

---

75 Mukhoty, Ira. *Akbar - The Great Mughal*. India. Aleph Book Company. April, 2020.

76 Ibid.

'It will pass. I suppose I spend too many long hours, tackling paperwork at my desk.' James smiled down at her.

'Not to mention the many late nights that you have to endure, attending all those parties and mehfils,' Khair teased him then. She knew James enjoyed socializing. 'I heard Chanda Bibi performed at the last one.'

'Yes,' James confirmed. 'I have to say that her dance is truly magical. It is no wonder she is so widely revered.' It was rumoured that the British officer, John Malcolm had recently been added to her list of admirers and that she was also quite taken with him.[77] Malcolm had even candidly expressed his ardent appreciation for her, specifically mentioning that he found the courtesan "a most remarkable woman."

'Anyhow, back to your grandfather. It is hardly surprising that a genteel, congenial man like him is well liked in the Company. He is popular with the ladies too. And do not forget that not very long ago, he was a dear friend to me as well.' James looked wistful for a moment and Khair gently reached out for his hand. She always seemed to know exactly what to do to comfort him. They started walking again, the balmy night air, warm on their faces. It was the beginning of summer and the city was much too hot during the day. The nights however, were considerably more pleasant. 'So, like I was saying,' continued James then. 'We cannot be complacent. This peaceful, uneventful time that we are enjoying might just be a brief interlude. It might even be the calm before the storm.'

'The calm before the storm, the calm before the storm!'

---

77 Interview with Salma Hussain, Noted Food Historian and Persian Scholar. May, 2022.

They both looked around, startled at the high-pitched screech, and then Khair pointed to a mango tree on the left. 'It is that parakeet again,' she commented about the sudden intrusion. 'The one with the blue crest and yellow beak. Always eavesdropping, that one! If it had not been for him, you would most certainly have kissed me that first night.'

They both burst into laughter at that and James couldn't help thinking that when she laughed, Khair really did look like a very young girl, almost child-like.

'I am sure he is listening even now.' James smiled indulgently toward the tree. He loved his pigeons, as did Khair, but there was something remarkable about parakeets. They really were extraordinarily sharp.

'Well, he ought to know that eavesdroppers never hear any good about themselves,' said Khair. 'Although, I suppose they really cannot help it. Parakeets are naturally keen listeners and they are very sharp too. It is one of their special characteristics.'

'Then you do know who else has that particular special characteristic, eh?'

Khair turned at the sudden grave tone. At that moment, the moon swiftly moved behind a cloud and the garden was thrown into abrupt darkness. Instinctively, she reached out for him. Encircling her waist with his arms, he pulled her close, so close that his lips were brushing against her earlobe. Then he leaned over and whispered.

'Mir Alam. He is a very keen listener too. And sharp, oh so sharp. I am telling you again Khair, we must be careful of him, very careful indeed.'

In fact, it was Baqar-Ali-Khan who posed the immediate problem.[78] Even while Mir Alam was still in prison, most likely trying to find a way to negotiate his release, Khair's grandfather decided to take things into his own hands. The truth was that he'd had a very hard time ever since the affair between James and Khair had started and things had been far from peaceful in his life. To think that his granddaughter, the fatherless girl he had cared for and supported, had blatantly disregarded his feelings by refusing to marry the man he had chosen for her, even going as far as to tell everyone that she would rather kill herself than be with a man she so loathed. The impudence of the girl! Not only was she bringing utter shame on the family, but she had made him, her grandfather, the laughing stock of his community. And that Kirkpatrick! He'd considered him a friend, a brother, he'd even trusted him enough to bring him into the zenana and introduce him to his family. He'd honoured him. And what had he done in return? Disgraced the very man who had shown him so much respect.

Then there was that investigation. The less said about it, the better! Who would have thought that it would be dropped like this, like a hot potato! Over and finished almost as soon as it had started. What tricks had Kirkpatrick played to make that happen? Which doors had he knocked on? What favours had he called in? Baqar didn't have any of the answers, but he did know one thing. It had all been unfair, grossly unfair.

They said they were in love! Pooh! A load of nonsense it was, the whole 'cannot-live-without-you' charade. A young, beautiful

78 Chancey, Marla Karen. In the Company's Secret Service. Thesis. Florida State University Library. 2003.

girl like his granddaughter and an older, senior British officer. Only a fool would not be able to understand what had steered them toward each other.

But he was no fool, he thought to himself one evening as he sat alone in his study after dinner. He could see right through them, could understand their depraved motivations. Shaking his head, Baqar refilled his fourth glass of Syrah. He needed to think with a calm, relaxed mind. Had he really earned the kind of respect and esteem few can, only to be tossed aside and shamed in his old age? Was he to become a mere pawn in the hands of his fifteen-year old granddaughter and a British officer who he had trusted? Undoubtedly, he would have to renounce the world, relinquish all associations and turn into a *fakir,* the only way to save his family from this disgrace. Was this...this shame going to become his fate? Was there nothing he could do to reign in a situation that was fast spiralling out of his control?

The situation couldn't be impossible, nothing ever was. After all, if Kirkpatrick could knock on doors, call in favours, then he could do the same. Despite the hard times that had befallen him, there were still many in the Company who sympathized with him.

The last time, Mir Alam had made a complaint. This time, he, Baqar, would do it. He'd endured enough, procrastinated enough. And of course, Kirkpatrick wasn't all that popular with everyone. There were many in the Company who resented him, even hated him. Any complaint against him would surely be taken seriously. Everyone knew his primary responsibility was to ensure cordial relations between the Company and the Hyderabadis, but if a complaint was made, alleging that his actions were creating disharmony, it would most certainly compel his superiors to apply pressure. Then Kirkpatrick would have no choice but to remove himself from the situation. Then the rumours would be dismissed as idle gossip, Khair would have to marry the young man her grandfather had chosen for her and things would return to the way they had always been in his palace. And so, having made up his mind, Baqar-Ali-Khan finished the Syrah and went to bed with an easy heart for the first time in months.

10
Ticking of the Clock

The summer days were usually long but that year, they seemed to have acquired an oddly rapid pace, as though time itself had assumed an inexplicable sense of urgency. Sometimes Khair couldn't help wishing that it would slow down, just a little bit, just enough to allow her to draw a breath, think coherently, gather her thoughts into something, anything that made some sort of sense. The nights, on the other hand, though shorter, seemed to stretch endlessly while she tossed and turned for hours in her intricately carved domed bed, trying to find a comfortable position. But try as she might, sleep wouldn't come and she'd sigh with exasperation and throw off the *razai*, before rushing to the window. She'd then fling it open, hoping for a breeze, but on those nights, even the air outside seemed inert and passive, made listless still from the state her mind was in.

She'd never thought that that evening in the garden outside his study when they'd spoken about Mir Alam and her grandfather, would be one of their last times together. The weeks after had a nightmarish quality to them. He hadn't even tried to see her after that, he'd simply sent a letter. A letter that she'd torn open with a beating heart and shaking hands. A letter that had brought her world crashing down almost as soon as she'd started reading. The tears that had instantly flooded her eyes had actually made it difficult for her to read the last lines, but she'd persisted, endured, right until his final goodbye. Clutching the letter in one hand and her chest with the other, her breath coming in short, urgent gasps, she'd then rushed straight into her mother's arms.

Later she'd cursed them. All of them. Mir Alam and that Wellesley, even her grandfather. All of them who thought they were powerful enough, big enough, mighty enough, almost as though they were god himself who could determine and command what should happen in the lives of other people. Hadn't they ever loved? Or been loved in return? Why couldn't they understand how her heart melted when she looked into those blue eyes, so much like the colour of the Hyderabad sky that she loved? Or how her arms ached to hold him during nights that had suddenly become painfully long. She'd cursed them, cursed them all to her heart's content, until she could curse no more. Afterward, she cursed herself, blamed herself for closing her eyes and falling so deeply in love that despite knowing the perils of the situation, she just hadn't been able to wrench herself out of it. At that moment, a futility had taken over her senses, a futility so bleak that it swept away every shred of hope that she'd previously clung to, making her wonder whether ending her life might really be the only option now.

And then this had happened. This inconceivable situation that she'd found herself in. At first, she'd simply thought that it had been the shock of it all, that the separation and the heartbreak had taken a toll. Then the anxiety, sleeplessness and loss of appetite had set in. Within days, she'd lost the energy to go for her daily stroll in the courtyard outside. She didn't even want to join the other women for hookah and cards in the garden. There were days when she'd simply sit for hours in her favourite armchair by the window, staring listlessly up at the sky outside. Sometimes her gaze would shift to the Charminar. It always looked different depending on the time of day. Mellow in the early morning, brighter in the harsher afternoon sun and luminescent in the waning evening light. The Jama Masjid and Mecca Masjid would be there too, magnificent in their timeless architectural splendor. Khair knew that the former was almost as old as the Charminar and like its name suggested, the first mosque to have been built in the area. The Mecca Masjid on the other hand, had taken nearly seventy-seven years to complete. It was said that construction had started back in 1614 and the sixth king of the Qutb Shahi dynasty, Sultan Mohammad Qutb Shah had even laid the foundation stone himself, but legend had it that whoever would complete the work of the mosque would have to accept the end of his dynasty. The result was that the work dragged on and it was finally completed in 1694, by the Mughal ruler Aurangzeb, almost seventy-seven years after it had been started.[79] Now, all these decades later, it really did seem as though time must have stopped back then for the beautiful stone structure.

'Unlike me,' muttered Khair to herself now as she thought about it. She'd been feeling particularly melancholy today. 'In my case, it seems to be galloping at lightning speed.' Normally she wouldn't even have noticed, but these days, time really did matter. After all, the constant ticking of the clock, the passing of the days, then weeks, had only resulted in confirming what had started out as a niggling doubt, into something that would inevitably change the course of her life. Something that would either bind them together forever or

79 Interview and tour with Mr. S Anand, Registered Guide, Dept of Tourism, Govt of Telangana. January, 2022.

completely tear them apart. Closing her eyes, she placed her right hand on her belly. It wouldn't be noticeable to anyone for a while, but she could already feel it. The slightest swell, so slight in fact, that it was almost indiscernible. Yet, it was discernible enough to tell her that she couldn't deny it, couldn't refute it any longer. Yes, now she knew it without a shadow of doubt. She was definitely, most certainly, pregnant with James's child.[80]

If the affair had evoked the kind of disapproval and condemnation that it had, then Khair could just imagine the disgrace and shame that she'd be subjected to when news about this illegitimate pregnancy got around. There was however, the other option too. It was not encouraged of course, in fact it was not permitted in most cases, but her circumstances were different.[81] And the choices were plentiful. Bloodletting, wild herbs and leaves, intense fasting and fumigation, pouring hot water on the abdomen. All she had to do was choose the one she fancied the most.

Khair shuddered. The zenanas were rife with horrific stories about attempted abortions that had gone wrong and young women who had perished and died in the process. Needless to say, it was not a situation that Khair wanted to put herself in. Besides, this was a child conceived out of the deep love that James and she had for each other. A love that would have blossomed, had it not been for men like her grandfather and Mir Alam, who had used her and James as mere pawns in their quest for honour and power.

Her family though, wouldn't care about all that. They would only think about the ruin, the shame this would bring on them.

---

80 Laslocky, Megan. *The Little Book of Heartbreak: Love gone wrong through the ages.* USA. Plume, a member of Penguin Group, USA. January, 2013.

81 Interview with Salma Hussain, Noted Food Historian and Persian Scholar. May, 2022.

The pressure they would apply would be undoubtedly, tremendous. But, if they could be heartless and brutal, then she could be equally resolute and unyielding. After all, this was her life, her decision. And she loved James, more than anyone. Why should she not have his baby? With a determined look, much like the one James had seen on her face the first time she had approached him in the garden behind his study, Khair then walked over to the sheesham table by her bed. The bowl of dates looked inviting and reaching for it, she plucked out a handful. The purifying fruit offered in paradise. The symbol of triumph, faith and abundance. Even as she bit into one and smiled to herself, she couldn't think of a more appropriate way to acknowledge and welcome the child she was carrying in her womb and would give birth to, seven months from now.

If the passage of time had seemed much too fast to Khair, it was the same on the other side of town. To James also, it felt as though the clock was ticking too fast and things were rapidly spiraling out of his control. Unlike Khair though, James wasn't close to any major decisions. In fact, a sense of uncertainty started settling within him as the months passed and sometimes he would just sit in his study for hours, thinking, wondering, musing over how and when he seemed to have handed over the reins of his life to other people. After those complaints had been made against him, he had been forced into giving her up, and the heartbreak he had suffered over losing her was difficult to explain to anyone. Then, there was the intense pressure that he was being subjected to from Calcutta about a treaty that the Governor General wanted the Nizam to sign. Wellesley wanted the British forces to be increased by 2000 infantry and 1000 cavalry, along with certain provinces. Negotiations had been going on for several months, but Wellesley seemed to be rapidly losing patience with James.

Ultimately, after months of intense negotiations, the much-anticipated treaty between the Company and the Nizam was signed.[82] Wellesley was happy at last and the Nizam bestowed another title on James, this time in fact, a very special one – Farzand Mohabat Paivand, i.e. Beloved son.[83] At that time, it must have seemed to many that James's luck was finally turning around, but contrary to what others believed, James was now more than ever before, riddled with guilt and a deepening sense of heartache that tore at him, sandwiched him between two sides that were equally dear to him. And of course, deep down he knew that despite the treaty, despite everything that he might do, the Governor General and he did not see eye-to-eye and probably never would. In fact, sometimes James couldn't help but wonder whether it would finally come to Wellesley replacing him with someone else or James resigning himself. Really, was this the price he had to pay for trying to survive in a world that he no longer recognized?

He was sitting in his study one evening, poring over some paperwork. The weather had been better for weeks and autumn had already started wrapping her cool, crisp arms around the city. The flower gardens, tree-lined streets and river banks were a brilliant potpourri of colours, bursting with golden beauty, but for James, it was simply unbelievable how quickly time had passed. Had it already been a year since that evening when he'd watched the leaves change colour from this window, and wondered about the repercussions of

82 Fuhr, Enid M. Thesis on Strategy and Diplomacy in British India Under Marquis Wellesley. King's College, University of London, 1988.

83 Ali Khan, Raza. Hyderabad 400 Years. Hyderabad, India. Zenith Services. 1991.

his decisions, about what the future had in store for them? So much had happened, so much had changed since then.

There was a tentative knock at the door and James looked up from his desk. 'Yes?'

His butler stepped in, looking slightly hesitant. 'I am sorry sir, but Dr Ure is here to see you. He said you are expecting him.'

'Oh yes!' James slapped his forehead with his hand. Talk about being forgetful! What was happening to him?

Turning to the butler, he nodded. 'Please escort the Doctor to the resting room. I will be there in a few moments.'

'Very well, sir.' The butler retreated and James rose from his desk. He'd been sitting there for several hours and wanted to freshen up before he met Dr Ure.

True to his word, five minutes later, he was with Dr Ure. Other than being the Residency doctor, Dr Ure was also a trusted friend and James knew that he truly cared for the Residency staff, often going far beyond his call of duty. Now, after a brief physical examination, Dr Ure pulled out a thermometer from his bag and slipped it into James's mouth. After checking his temperature, he put the thermometer away and then looked at James gravely. 'Well, your temperature is normal. Though you seem to have lost more weight since the last time I saw you. Are you eating the broth I had prescribed?'

James smiled. 'Every day. Although sometimes it is difficult to keep it down.'

The doctor smiled back at him. 'It is too bland for your taste, eh? You would much rather prefer the eggplant curry?' he asked, referring to James's favourite Hyderabadi dish.

James laughed then. 'I have little appetite these days for most of the things.'

The doctor looked concerned at the remark. 'How frequent are the headaches?'

'Quite,' answered James honestly. He didn't tell the doctor that sometimes they were so bad, it felt as though he had a heartbeat inside his head.

'Hmm. Perhaps a change of scene? It will take your mind off things.'

James nodded slowly, thinking over the doctor's suggestion. The festival of *Urs* was around the corner and it might do him good to get away from the city for a few days. He always enjoyed the local festivals and even though Urs was a Sufi festival, it was widely attended and celebrated by Hindus and Muslims alike.[84] People in huge numbers set off from the city every year, on a pilgrimage to the shrine of Maula Ali.

'I think that might be a good idea,' he agreed, looking happier than he had in a long time. 'Some fresh air will do me good. I will ask Aziz Ullah to make the arrangements. In the meantime, can you prescribe something for the headaches?'

Dr Ure opened his bag and pulled out a bottle filled with a cloudy, colorless syrup. 'This should help,' he said as he wrote out a prescription and handed the bottle to James. 'A spoonful every night, preferably after supper. And I know you have adopted many of the local ways, but please do not go to any of those hakims[85] with

84 Interview with Diwan Gautam Anand. Famed Sufi Poet, Hotelier, Author and Food Connoisseur. January, 2022.

85 Saini, Anu. *Physicians of Colonial India.* National Library of Medicine, India. July – Sept, 2016.

their *Unani* medicines that they use in the old city. The eggplant,' he added then, stroking his chin thoughtfully, 'now that, I have nothing against.'

They both laughed and then the doctor picked up his bag and rose from his chair. 'You might want to tell your valet to go ahead and pack your bags. The clock is ticking.'

'Is it ever?' James couldn't help wondering aloud as he walked the doctor out.

11
Chosen Paths

During his time in India, particularly Hyderabad, James had observed many differences between the Hindus and the Muslims. However, decades of intermingling also meant that both communities had imbibed customs and traditions from each other.[86] This was true of festivals as well. While several of the festivals were observed and celebrated together, there were few that seemed to have an appeal as universal as the Sufi festival of Urs. Legend had it that Sufism first came to India as early back as the twelfth century, when Khwaja Muinuddin Chisti came to Lahore from Ghazni and settled in Ajmer.[87] Of course, over time, customs and traditions were gradually Indianized, since that was a unique characteristic of India. India was like a mosaic; she would take the best from anyone who came to her and make it her own.

Like everything else that came to India, Islam too adapted to local ways and practices. Sufism particularly, with its teachings of brotherhood, inclusivity and equal treatment for all, became widely popular. The Sufis were mystics who focused on the inner pursuit

86 Interview with Salma Yusuf Hussain. Food Historian and Persian Scholar. May, 2022.

87 Interview with Diwan Gautam Anand. Famed Sufi Poet, Hotelier, Author and Food Connoisseur. January, 2022.

of the Almighty, compassion toward all fellow human beings and the shunning of materialism. In fact, in that sense they were much like the Hindu saints. With its simple teachings, easy practices and focus on tolerance, Sufism was considered neutral and even accommodating enough to imbibe customs from other religions, including the popular *bhakti* movement, like offering flowers or coconut at the *dargah.* Of course, music also played a major role in this. Music had always been an integral part of Indian customs and Sufi devotional singing quickly became the rage. The term "sa'ma" which means "to listen" was a form of worship, and combined singing, playing instruments, dancing, recitation of poetry and prayers. There was a mystical quality to the tradition which instantly appealed to everyone. It wasn't surprising then that a very diverse mix of people was always to be found at the dargah and this was proof of the seamless way in which the adaption into the indigenous culture had happened.[88] And nothing brought the people of Hyderabad together like the festival of Urs. It was widespread in its appeal to all – *Sunnis, Shias,* Hindus. The Nizam of course was Sunni, as were the *Paigahs.* The Paigahs who were considered next only to the Nizams in aristocratic hierarchy in Hyderabad, were responsible for the defence of the state and were great patrons of art as well. The "Paigah" title had actually been bestowed by the second Nizam of Hyderabad on Nawab Abul Fateh Taig Jung Bahadur. Abul Fateh Khan who was fiercely loyal to the Nizam, then went on to become the originator of the Paigah clan. Of course, Hyderabad also had a huge Shia population, as well as a sizeable number of Hindus. And Urs was an example of how a festival could unite people,

88 Interview with Diwan Gautam Anand. Famed Sufi Poet, Hotelier, Author and Food Connoisseur. January, 2022.

irrespective of their origins or religions. Hundreds of people set off every year on a pilgrimage to the shrine of Maula Ali, and celebrated the occasion with fervour and devotion. Even the courtesans of the city, including Chanda Bibi, always participated enthusiastically in the festivities. The singing, dancing, eating and revelling gave the festival a cultural feeling rather than simply religious and made it popular not only among the Muslims and the Hindus, but also among the British, especially those like James. He eagerly looked forward to the celebrations every year, but this time his reasons were different. This year, Urs was not merely a festival to James, it was a respite, a means to get away from the difficult and nerve-wracking situation that seemed to have engulfed him in Hyderabad.

While James was away, Khair had been confined to the zenana palace in her grandfather's deorhi. If regular news had a way of getting around, then the news of an illegitimate pregnancy moved at a very rapid pace indeed. Not surprisingly, the pressure to abort the child had been tremendous on her, but she had remained resolute and hadn't been swayed by any of it.[89] Nothing had dissuaded her; neither the emotional threats, nor the intimidation.

'For a girl that young, she is very stubborn,' one of her uncles had remarked furiously to her mother when Khair had bluntly refused to go through the abortion, even expressing outrage at being pressured into marrying a man for whom she felt such revulsion. 'She does not even care about the disgrace, the dishonour that this child will bring on all of us. It is appalling!'

---

89 Chancey, Marla Karen. "In the Company's Secret Service." Thesis, Florida State University Library. 2003.

'She is in love with the Englishman.' Her mother had even smiled slightly, inwardly proud of her daughter's resilience and determined to support her. 'There is nothing appalling about being in love.'

'She is a Sayyida.' The man's tone had become dangerously low. 'That man is a Christian. He is...'

'A high-ranking officer in the Company.' Sharaf-un-Nissa had looked at him pointedly as she completed the sentence for him. 'And, might I add, the Nizam's beloved son.' She shot the now silent man a triumphant look. 'Anyhow, I think the time to discuss this is over. You know what the *hadith*[90] says. There is no point now.' She was referring to the fact that Khair was already several months into her pregnancy and according to the hadith, the foetus becomes a living soul after 120 days of gestation. 'That ship has sailed,' she concluded then with a wave of her hand. She knew she was talking as much about the abortion as about Khair's marriage to the boy Baqar-Ali-Khan had chosen. With Khair already several months pregnant, that was out of the question. Perhaps that was a good thing? But what were the other options? The last thing she wanted was for her daughter to give birth to an illegitimate child and live in her grandfather's mansion as an unwed and disgraced woman! Khair didn't deserve that. She deserved so much more, a husband who loved her, wealth and status, respect and legitimacy. 'There are other things to think about now,' concluded Sharaf-un-Nissa then with a firm nod.

She did not see the need to tell him what those were. The truth was that Sharaf-un-Nissa was well aware of the fact that the

---

90 A collection of traditions containing sayings of the prophet Muhammad which, with accounts of his daily practice (the Sunna), constitute the major source of guidance for Muslims, apart from the Koran.

one person standing in the way of Khair's happiness was her own grandfather. He was going around, touting to everyone how he had been victimized and humiliated, trying to get sympathy from anyone who cared to listen to his rants. And there were certainly some who were falling for it, both among the Hyderabadis as well as from within the Company. The two lovers were being pressurised to break off their relationship, to never see each other again. In fact, there had even been some talk about the investigation against Hushmat Jung being reopened.

It wasn't fair. After all, there were many examples of these sorts of marriages and they'd been so successful too. Take that General William Palmer for instance.[91] A good man with a lovely wife. What was her name now? Faiz Baksh[92], was it not? She was supposed to be a royal princess and a descendant of Shah Jahan himself.[93] And what beautiful children Palmer and she had. Faiz was older than Khair, but she was Persian too with an Indian mother, just like Khair. The lady was leading a fine, luxurious life and had even been bestowed with multiple titles after her marriage to the General. Sharaf-un-Nissa had heard that the General really doted on her and she had been accustomed to living in the greatest comfort with people constantly at her beck and call. Who wouldn't want that for her daughter? Why couldn't the old man understand? And what right did he have, to interfere in a matter that did not concern him? Yes, he had given them a home in his palace after Khair's father had died, but that did not give him the right to choose a husband for Khair!

91 Marshall, P.J. *Eighteenth Century India.* Oxford Dictionary of National Biography. May, 2005.

92 Portrait of Major William Palmer and his Family. Asian and African Studies Blog, British Library, 18 January 2015.

93 Fais Begum Faiz Palmer. Geni. Genealogy.

It was ridiculous! It was the father who had the right to do that, and after the father, it was the mother. And Sharaf-un-Nissa had already chosen.

The temperature seemed to have dropped considerably on the evening James returned to Hyderabad. Even as his palanquin came to a stop outside the portico of the Residency and he stepped into the building, he couldn't help thinking that despite the time away, he did not feel as refreshed and rejuvenated as he had hoped to. Yes, the fresh air had been good for him, but he hadn't been able to stop thinking about Khair-un-Nissa the entire time that he was there. Images of her lovely face and dark, earnest eyes had clouded his vision, sometimes even to the point of blocking out all rational thought. There were times when he'd wondered if he had made a terrible mistake by sending her that letter. Then again, the pressure of holding on to a relationship that was causing both of them such agony was too much, even for a determined man like him. It was all very bemusing though and the indecisiveness sometimes kept him awake long into the nights as he just lay there in his tent, listening to the revelries outside and wondering how he could extricate himself from a situation that seemed so impossible.

He tried not to dwell on it as he walked across the main hall and then turned toward his study. It was a chilly evening and he was glad that he'd chosen to wear his double-breasted, grey, beaver wool coat. The dense felted fabric unfailingly managed to keep the elements at bay, but today, James had even buttoned the collar up high to protect his ears and the back of his neck. He'd been running a fever since the day before and after the weight he'd recently lost, the early winter chill seemed to permeate his body more than usual.

His study though was warm and he was able to unfasten the top buttons on the coat as he entered the room and then glanced at some of the paperwork that had piled up on his desk during his time away. He knew that he was now behind in his work and despite the persisting headaches and fever, would have to put in extra time to sort through the backlog. Sighing, he quickly sifted through the letters, his sharp eyes separating the ones that he knew needed his urgent attention. There was one from William Palmer and one from the Governor General as well. These two, he pulled out of the pile and then placed them carefully on the side, before glancing through the sheaf again. That's when he saw it. The envelope wasn't the type he used himself, but the elegant Persian lettering was one that he instantly recognized. Despite the fact that he could hardly wait to tear the envelope open and read the contents of the letter, James took a moment to run his fingers across the thin paper, closing his eyes as he tried to imagine and savour the feel of the hands that had held it not very long back. Those long, gentle fingers that seemed to infuse a magic into whatever they touched. He could almost feel them now, caressing his back after they'd made love, threading their way through his hair, entwined in his as they strolled around the flower garden on a moonlit night, hand-in-hand. With a deep breath, James opened his eyes, consciously trying to tear himself away from thoughts that were urging him, tempting him, pulling him back on the path that he had tried to leave behind.

Silently admonishing himself for allowing his thoughts to get the better of him, James reached for the paper knife. Slicing the envelope open, he pulled out the single sheet of paper and unfolded it. The letter was written in Persian, the words joined neatly together in a cursive style. James of course, could read Persian and Hindoostani as well as he could read English and now his eyes scanned the single page quickly as he wondered what had compelled her to write to him after all these months. Though it was unlike her, this time she hadn't bothered with pleasantries and his question was answered almost immediately. Eyes widening, he had to clutch his chest with his free hand as he finished reading the letter that Khair had written to him, telling him that she was several months pregnant with his child. Pregnant! She was pregnant with his child! As the enormity of her words started slowly sinking in, James fell back into the dark brown, leather desk chair that he spent hours in every day. Whatever his earlier thoughts, he knew that this letter had now changed everything. Decisions, dilemmas, difficulties be damned, she was carrying his child! Even as he turned his head toward the flower garden where they'd strolled together so often, he saw that the vista outside had darkened considerably. At this late hour, the moonflowers that they both loved were in full bloom and as James sniffed their heady fragrance that was wafting in through the crack in the window, he knew with the utmost certainty that however riddled it might be with adversities, he was now back on the path that led to her, the path that would never allow him to abandon the woman he loved and the child she was carrying.

12
The Final Condition

With Khair-un-Nissa now pregnant with his child, James knew that he could no longer continue to deny his association with her, at least not to his brother. He was still not ready to tell him everything, nor was he in a position to include him in his future plans. Nevertheless, he knew he had to confess the truth about the affair to William. He understood that William would not be happy; he had already made his disapproval clear[94], particularly since the investigation. It actually felt strange to James, this constant resistance that he seemed to be up against. After all, so many others had been in the same boat, hadn't they? Palmer was one example, but even William himself was deeply involved with his Indian mistress, Dhoolaury. And it wasn't just a passing affair, it was evident how much his brother truly cared about her. And then there was that famous English lawyer, William Hickey. He'd married a local bibi called Jemdanee[95] though their story had been rather tragic since she'd died in childbirth after bearing him a son. Hickey who had always referred to her as his "cheerful and sweet-tempered Jemdanee", had been completely heartbroken after

94 Laslocky, Megan. *The Little Book of Heartbreak: Love gone wrong through the ages.* USA. Plume, a member of Penguin Group, USA. January, 2013.

95 An Indian Lady. National Gallery of Ireland. Online Collection.

her death.[96] Anyway, it did prove that regardless of changing norms and customs, in spite of greater prejudices and biases, inter-racial marriages weren't quite that uncommon. What then, was so sinful, so wrong, about what Khair and he had done?

Even as he started writing the letter to his brother, along with a feeling of trepidation, James did also experience immense relief. That was a result of the choice he had finally made. In spite of all the hardships that he knew they would have to endure, he felt as though a huge weight had been lifted off his heart. Envisioning a life without Khair had been agony and after all the indecision and uncertainty, he was actually thankful that destiny seemed to have stepped in and decided for them.

He did not tell William that, of course. He admitted the truth about the affair to him, told him about how it had all started and that he hadn't been able to hold himself back. The rest he kept to himself – the momentous turn of events in his life, the decision he now intended to take, the path he had chosen. At that point, the ink had blotted the pristine white paper. James had pressed too hard into the sheet as he'd stopped to think about the enormity of the situation. After all, it no longer was a matter of choice or even just a matter of love; it was now a matter of honour and integrity. James was well aware that there would be many who would turn against him again. He had seen that in the past too. They would condemn him, pull him down, perhaps even try to destroy him. The truth was that he had been unable to rest or sleep as he wondered what lay ahead for him and the incessant worrying had indeed taken a toll on his health. So much so, that thoughts about resigning from

---

96 R. Farr, James. *Who was William Hickey? A Crafted Life in Georgian England and Imperial India.* U.S.A. Routledge. 26 Sep 2019.

his post had recently crossed his mind several times, but admitting that to William was another matter. William was the one who had been instrumental in the position of Resident being offered to James. He was the one who had supported, even facilitated James's appointment. But what if resigning might be the only option now? James couldn't refute something that was fast becoming a very real possibility. Abandoning Khair was unthinkable, now that he knew she was carrying his child. He would never be able to convince his conscience to do that, however much he tried. And deep in his heart, James knew that other than being a matter of honour and conscience, there was another compelling reason that had driven him to take the decision. For besides the intense love he felt for Khair, a bond had also now formed between his unborn child and him, the child that was a part of him, the child that he already loved. The child that he could never desert.

Despite having taken his decision, James had no way of knowing how quickly things would suddenly begin to move for Khair and him. Ironically, it all started with some very distressing news. James had always known Baqar-Ali-Khan to be a charming, affable man, but he hadn't been aware of how determined and dogged he could be, particularly when it came to a matter that concerned his family honour. He also seemed to have a way with the high-ranking officials in the Company because his complaints were taken very seriously and he was actually successful in getting the investigation against James, reopened. This time, however, he didn't limit the allegations to the affair. He actually claimed that the Resident had been using intimidation, threats and coercion to get what he wanted. It was a very serious accusation and would most certainly ruin James's career as well as his life, if proven. The worst thing was that there were plenty of people who were inclined to believe Baqar, and it soon became clear that James would be assumed guilty unless he could prove otherwise. At that point, it felt to James as though he was caught in the middle of what felt like a vortex that wanted to engulf him, absorb him, finish him. Now all he could do was hope and pray that somehow, someone would come forward and help him prove his innocence.

With a practiced hand, Sharaf-un-Nissa removed the veil that had securely covered her head and today, even her face. She was aware though that in some of the strictest zenanas, the veil wouldn't have been enough and any male visitor would have to be covered from head to foot in a shroud and led blindly to the lady, accompanied by a eunuch. In any case, male visitors were rare in the zenana except on account of an urgent situation. The visit a while ago, did qualify as urgent. Obviously, she'd followed protocol and met the visitor from behind a screen, but even so, the veil had stayed on throughout the very brief meeting. A meeting which had gone just as she'd wanted it to. After all, this was what she'd hoped for, prayed for. One chance, one opportunity to turn things around in her daughter's favour. And she'd done it. The die had been cast. There was no turning back now. Of course, there would be some who would call her dishonourable, even question her morality and loyalty to her own people. But, she was a mother. She had every right to do whatever it took to ensure her child's happiness. And so, she had. Nodding to herself, as though satisfied, she made a swift turn towards Khair's room.

The afternoon sun was strong even on this cold December day and the room was flooded with bright, golden light. Squinting, Sharaf-un-Nissa raised her hand to shield her eyes from the sunrays as she looked around for her daughter. For a moment, she didn't even see her, the sunlight too harsh. Then she spotted her and almost instantly smiled to herself. Khair was sitting in her preferred spot, but this time instead of her favourite chair, she had asked one of the maids to pull the velvet divan over by the window. In this late stage of pregnancy, she'd been advised to rest her legs as much as she could. Now she had a contemplative look on her face as she sat there on the divan, legs stretched out, her left hand placed under her chin while the right one rested on the bodice of her embroidered kurta. She was almost seven months into her pregnancy, but even in her current state, Khair looked beautiful. In fact, there was an undeniable grace and elegance about her that few women possessed. 'No wonder the Englishman cannot see beyond her,' Sharaf-un-Nissa murmured to herself as she tossed the discarded veil onto the bed and strode over to her daughter.

'Khair Joon?'

Startled, Khair turned around. On seeing her mother there, she started to rise from the divan but Sharaf-un-Nissa put a hand up to stop her. 'Sit, sit. I have something to tell you.' She joined her daughter on the divan and then looked at her with concern. 'Would you like something to eat? You must take care of yourself during this time.' Then her face brightened. 'Two crates of oranges and apples came in from the Residency yesterday. Would you like some? I have to say, he is a very caring and considerate gentleman, that one,' she added as Khair blushed. James had been very attentive toward her recently. Ever since he'd known about the pregnancy, huge quantities of fruits, dry fruits and other delicacies had been regularly coming in from the Residency.

Khair smiled. 'I will eat in a while. I ate too much at lunch. The *Shikampuri Kebabs* were very tender today.'

'It is not surprising,' said her mother then. 'Your uncle has lost another tooth. The khansama has been instructed to pound the meat until it becomes a melt-in-the-mouth paste.'

'Uncle will lose all his teeth soon. Why does he not give up his habit of chewing betelnut all day?' Khair shook her head and laughed. Then her expression became sombre. 'There is something on your mind Maman Joon. I can tell.'

'We know each other very well, my child.' Moving closer to her daughter, Sharaf-un-Nissa covered Khair's hand with hers. The torments, the anguish, the agony that she had gone through over the last few months would surely have been enough to break the spirit of most young women. But not Khair. No, Khair wasn't like anyone else. Such a young girl, yet she displayed so much strength and resilience. 'Things have lately been hard for both of you, have they not?' Khair knew her mother was referring to James and she lowered her eyes, nodding slightly. They had started meeting again, but with the amount of trouble the scandal had caused them both, they were still trying to be as discreet as they could. And now with the new allegations and the investigation having been opened again, things had started looking extremely uncertain.

'Someone came to see me today.'

Khair looked up in surprise at this sudden change in subject. They often had visitors at the palace, it was a common occurrence. But by the tone of her mother's voice, Khair could tell that this hadn't been just any usual visitor. She waited for her mother to continue.

'It was about the investigation that has been reopened against Hushmat Jung. Apparently, they are taking a serious view of it since there has been an allegation about force and threats being used.'

'A serious view!' Khair looked instantly agitated. 'It is all nonsense! It is all Nana's fault. Him and Mir Alam and those racist bigots in the Company who cannot bear to see James and me together.'

'Do not get distressed, my dear.' Sharaf-un-Nissa patted Khair's hand. 'It is not good to get excited in this condition. In any case, they came here because they wanted me to confirm the allegations that your grandfather has made against the Resident.'

'And what did you say?' Khair stared at her mother with big, anxious eyes. She had complete faith in her, but coercion and intimidation were not rare, particularly with women.

'Well, obviously, I told them the truth. That Hushmat Jung is innocent.' Sharaf-un-Nissa shrugged, then smiled. 'I told them about your grandfather's senseless insistence to keep two people, who love each other to the point of distraction, apart. I told them that I as your mother, truly believe that you and Hushmat Jung are meant to be together and that it is my ardent wish to see you belong to the man you love.'

Khair looked at her mother in wonder. She was a woman! From where and how did she draw such tremendous strength, such fortitude to do and say what she believed was right, however difficult and perilous it might be.

'Do not look at me like that, Khair Joon. Just because we are women does not mean that we are destined to relinquish all the decisions of our lives to the men who supposedly rule us. I have never believed that and I hope that you never will either.' She smiled and wrapped her arm around Khair's shoulder. 'I do believe that Hushmat Jung's name has been cleared. Your grandfather now has no choice but to back down gracefully and accept what is to be.'

The sheer joy she then saw on her daughter's face brought instant tears to the mother's eyes. So many long months! How much this child of hers had borne! How much she had suffered! Now at last this agony, this wait would be over. However, she did know that despite things turning in their favour, there still remained one last hindrance that needed to be removed, one last requisite that needed to be fulfilled, one final condition without which none of this was possible. Even though it pained her to mention it now, she knew that for Khair's sake, she had to be brutally honest with her. The stakes were too high for her not to be.

'To see you married to that fine man who I know truly loves you, well... nothing would make me happier,' she repeated. 'However, you do know that there is one final condition that needs to be met? Without that, much as I may want to, even I cannot make any of this possible.'

'Yes Maman Joon, I know.' Khair nodded. They had always known that it would ultimately come to this.

'You are a Sayyida. You know what that means.' Sharaf-un-Nissa shook her head. 'I have done what I could. It is out of my hands now. And so, I truly wish for your sake, that he loves you enough to fulfil this last condition. I hope he loves you enough to make this sacrifice, to remove this last hindrance that still stands between the two of you. I really hope he does.'

13
Holy Words

The glittering chandeliers, the marble arches, the latticed windows, the carved domes, the fountains spouting crystal clear water, on any other day, the palace would have been magnificent on its own. However, just knowing that it wasn't any ordinary day, that it was the day of the younger granddaughter's wedding, was enough to make anyone wonder. Where were the hundreds of fairy lights? Why had the palace courtyard not been adorned with beautiful shamiana tents? Where was the dastarkhwan that should have been audibly groaning under the weight of an elaborate wedding feast? Where were the sounds of talking and laughing that should have rung out from every corner of the deorhi as hundreds of guests continued to pour in through the enormous double gates? Where was the celebration, the jubilation?

Growing up, Khair-un-Nissa had attended innumerable weddings and like any young woman from a noble family, she too had anticipated a grand wedding party for herself. Today, her marriage to James was going to take place according to Islamic rites[97] but the fact that Khair was more than seven months pregnant on the

---

97 Carlyle and "Irving's London Circle": *Some Unpublished Letters by Thomas Carlyle and Mrs. Edward Strachey.* Vol 69, No. 5 pp 1135-1149. J. Calder, Grace. Cambridge University Press. Dec 1954.

day of her wedding ensured that instead of an elaborate celebration, the wedding was an extremely quiet and private affair, attended only by those who absolutely needed to be there. To someone who did not know or understand the bride, the absence of the extravagant revelries that were usual in a wedding such as this, would have seemed like a major let down, an enormous disappointment. What they would never know was that for Khair, the fact that she was marrying the man she loved deeply, after months of waiting, wondering and imagining the worst, that joy truly was far beyond any happiness that any celebration could have brought. Dressed in the traditional zardozi khada dupatta with its elaborate kurta and matching veil, Khair looked resplendent. The *maang tikka,* jhoomar, *nath,* satlada, *guluband* and chandbalis were magnificent, but those who did know her could tell that it was the radiance on her face and the joy in her eyes, that truly made her the most beautiful bride they had ever seen.

If the wedding was going to be a small and intimate affair, then the conversion had been even more quiet and private.[98] A *maulvi* and two witnesses had been the only people present when James had taken the *Shahada.* This Islamic oath which James knew was a part of the *Adhan* and was considered one of "The Five Pillars of Islam", was a simple one, a single sentence that once spoken would declare his belief in the oneness of Allah and the acceptance of Muhammad as his messenger. Once this was done, the certificate on the letterhead of the mosque was issued and the process completed as quietly as

98 Malcolm, John. Private Secretary – Scandal in Hyderabad. Malcolm – Soldier, Diplomat, Ideologue of British India: The Life of Sir John Malcolm. UK. John Donald – An Imprint of Birlinn Ltd. 2014.

possible. Of course, the simplicity and swiftness of the conversion notwithstanding, James couldn't deny the enormity of the step he had just taken when the shahada certificate was handed over to him. He knew that some might call it a massive sacrifice. Others might call it surrender. Yet others might even consider it sacrilege. For him though, it was the inevitable final step that he'd known he would have to take, to be able to honour and cherish the only woman he truly loved. And he'd done it. James Achilles Kirkpatrick was now a Muslim and according to sharia law, his marriage to noblewoman Khair-un-Nissa would be a legally recognized one. And that was really all that mattered.

As was customary, the nikah took place in the home of the bride. Her grandfather's deorhi was the only home Khair had ever known and was naturally the chosen venue for the ceremony. Despite the fact that Baqar-Ali-Khan had now given his consent as well as opened the doors of his palace for the wedding, perhaps the humiliation and heartache that the affair had caused him was still too raw to allow him to personally participate. His absence was conspicuous, particularly since Khair did not have a father. Added to that was the starkness of the total absence of James's family. In an Islamic marriage, where the two fathers play the most prominent roles, this would not have gone unnoticed, but the participation of the Prime Minister himself was what salvaged the situation. Aristu Jah, who was openly ecstatic about the union was only too happy to stand in as adopted "father of the bride" and even bestowed her with expensive presents, including a share in his jagir, as was customary. The Nizam had always been very fond of James and considered him a son. It was therefore evident that in spite of the condemnation and defamation that the relationship had endured, it had now been generously blessed by those who occupied the highest positions of authority in Hyderabad.

Of course, despite the acceptance and support of the Hyderabadis, James's battles were far from over. He, in fact, had an excruciatingly long road ahead as far as the Company was concerned. The Governor General and several like him, had always been distrustful of the way James had adopted Indian customs and practices. Time and again, his love for the country of his birth had been conceived as a lack of loyalty for his own people. James was well aware of the fact that if rumours of his alleged association and affair with Khair could cause the kind of trouble they had, then news about his conversion to Islam and subsequent marriage to her, would likely be the end of everything that he had ever known. No, he couldn't tell anyone about it yet, not even his brother, with whom he had been more honest than with anyone else. It was one thing to tell his brother that he had fallen in love with a local noblewoman, but quite another to admit to his extreme step of converting to Islam in order to marry her. James knew that his conversion really had taken him too far. William would never understand it, and besides, James did not want to jeopardise William's future by telling him the truth. He did not want the cloud of suspicion that he had lived under for so long, to also cast its shadow on the brother he loved. It was just easier to carry on with the lies and the denial.

It was not surprising then, that in spite of now being legally married, marital bliss was still a distant dream for James and Khair. The most glaring sign of this heart-breaking reality was the absence of the elaborately decorated palanquin that should have been waiting at the entrance of Baqar-Ali-Khan's deorhi to take the bride to her husband's home. Instead, once the marriage contract was signed and the nikah completed, Khair stayed back in the deorhi and watched from one of its latticed windows as James got into his palanquin to make the journey back to the Residency on the other side of town. If the love that had finally led them to each other had been an extraordinary one, then the marriage that had now joined them together for life, wasn't an ordinary one either.

It was almost morning when Khair finally made it back to her bedroom. Entering the room, she closed the door behind her and then walked up to the gilded full-length mirror, as fast as her condition would allow. She then briskly reached for the bejewelled brooch on her left shoulder that held the khada dupatta in place. 'It really is as uncomfortable as it looks,' she said aloud to herself as she unpinned the brooch and then removed the dupatta. 'Even more so if the bride is seven months pregnant. But I suppose that does not happen all that often.' Laughing at her own audaciousness, she then proceeded to remove her jewellery. One by one, it all came off, until finally, she stood there in just the kurta and churidar, looking like the very young girl that she was. Even as she stared at her reflection in the mirror, she couldn't believe how everything could seem the same, when in fact, everything had changed.

Qubool hai, qubool hai! She could still clearly hear the two holy words that they'd both spoken that night, the two words that had concluded their nikah, binding them together for life. Cupping her face between her hennaed hands, Khair shook her head in wonder. It still seemed unbelievable to her. She was now married to James, she belonged to him. Naturally though, it hadn't been easy to accept the fact that she couldn't step into her new home yet, nor to see him get into his palanquin while she stayed behind in her grandfather's deorhi. But there had been no other option. Young though she was, she knew how perilous their situation was. People could be very cruel, very heartless. Who understood that better, than the two of them?

Turning away from the mirror, Khair walked over to the sheesham table beside her bed. As usual the maid had left on it, a silver tumbler filled to the brim with saffron milk. The saffron threads had become infused in the milk, giving it a luxurious, pale orange hue. Generously garnished with slivered almonds and cashews, the milk was a nightly ritual that her mother had asked her to follow ever since she'd known about the pregnancy. With a smile, Khair picked up the tumbler and got into bed. Despite the wedding being a private affair, the last few days had been frenetic. This in fact, was her first moment of quiet solitude and she wanted to savour every bit of it. Leaning back against the embroidered silk cushions, she sipped the beverage slowly, enjoying the velvety smoothness of the milk and the earthy yet sweet aroma of the saffron. Soon the sounds of the Adhan would be heard as the Muezzin recited from the mosque, summoning people for prayer. One Muezzin would begin the call, then another would join, then yet more, until the sounds of their multiple voices would reverberate around the entire city. Then the sun would rise and the city would come to life. The bazaars would open for their daily trade, the streets would fill up with bullock carts and fruit vendors, the *dhobi ghat* would resonate with the *chap-chap-chapaak* sounds of clothes being washed. Another ordinary day. Yet, for her, nothing about this day was ordinary. This day, which would mark an extraordinary new beginning in her life. This day that she would always remember as the day she had married the handsome Englishman. The one with the brilliant blue eyes, as brilliant as the sky itself. Even as she thought about him, a small smile started playing on her lips. 'Perhaps this really is our last test,' she thought out loud then. 'After all, we have already crossed the most difficult hurdles. Perhaps now, we really will be together forever.'

With that last thought and the two holy words still resonating in her ears, Khair finished her milk, gently placed the empty tumbler back on the table and then finally, slid deeper into the bed and closed her eyes.

14
Mir Ghulam Ali, Sahib Allum

He'd thought that he'd remember the day when he'd been given the Hyderabad posting as the happiest day of his life. After all, it had been the highest point in his career, a position which along with prestige and status, had brought with it the realization of a dream. Then, after all those long months of waiting and wondering, when he'd finally managed to marry the woman he loved, he'd thought that nothing would ever come close to that. The feeling of knowing that now Khair and he really did belong to each other. But it was 6 March 1801[99], a beautiful spring day in Hyderabad, that would go on to remain etched in his memory as the happiest, most joyous moment of his life. It was the day that James realized that there really was such a thing as complete happiness, a joy that is unmatched, unparalleled by every other. For that was the day when James became a father to a beautiful baby boy, a child who stole his heart from the moment he first laid eyes on him. The instant he held his new-born son in his arms for the very first time and looked into the eyes that were so much like his own, James knew with the utmost certainty that this was truly a moment, a love, like none he had ever known before.

---

99 William George Kirkpatrick (Mir Ghulam Ali Sahib Allum). Geni. Genealogy.

The baby was born in his great grandfather's deorhi with an army of *dais* and nurses present. Khair's mother and James were both there, though of course James's presence was rather unusual. There was no specific rule against the father being there; it just wasn't common practice. The delivery was uncomplicated enough though, and James was relieved that Khair had sailed through without too much difficulty. Immediately after the birth, the baby was cleaned and swaddled, before being handed over to his father. Then, as per tradition, James whispered the Adhan in his right ear and the *Iqamah* in his left. Afterwards, according to the *Tahneek*, a softened date was rubbed on his palate from left to right.[100] Other than being a ceremonial ritual, this would also exercise the muscles of the mouth and help with the circulation of blood. During the lifetime of the Prophet, Muslims used to bring their new-borns to him to perform the ritual. Now it was the father who did it. Finally, after all the rituals had been completed, the new parents proudly gave the baby the name they had chosen for him – Mir Ghulam Ali. 'It is a praiseworthy name indeed,' remarked relatives approvingly when they heard about it. Then when James went on to add the title of *Sahib Allum* to his son's name, it couldn't have been more appropriate. Mir Ghulam Ali, Sahib Allum, Lord of the Universe. And to them, he was. He really was.

The next few days were fraught with the frenetic activity that was usual after the birth of a child. Khair of course, was supposed to observe a forty-day *chilla* or confinement period[101] during which

100 Meehan, Sumayyah. Welcome a New Born to the Way of Faith. *Khaleej Times*. 16 May 2008.

101 Interview with Salma Yusuf Hussain, Food Historian and Persian Scholar. May, 2022.

she had plenty of time to rest and recoup her energy. Like other aristocratic women, she wouldn't be breastfeeding the baby, there were wet nurses for that, and James had even hired the finest *lori* singers from the city for his new-born son. He, in fact, as the father of the child, had several responsibilities to fulfil. One of the most important of these was the *aqiqah* on the seventh day, entailing the sacrifice of a few sheep or goats to be given to the poor. According to the hadith, at least two animals were to be sacrificed for a boy and this was the parents' way of thanking Allah for blessing them with a child. Then a feast was prepared, singers and dancers were hired and visitors were welcomed into the deorhi to bless the new baby. They came bearing gifts of clothes, toys, sweetmeats and jewellery. Among the many guests who came was the Prime Minister himself and even the Nizam sent his blessings with presents from the Chowmahallah Palace for the new mother and child.

On the fortieth day after the birth, sweetmeats and dates were distributed among friends and family, and Khair's confinement period was officially declared over. She continued to stay at the deorhi, but James dutifully visited her and the baby every single day. He also unfailingly brought her something every time he came, sometimes it was things she liked to eat, other times he would stop over at one of the bazaars to buy the bangles she loved so much or a pair of silver anklets. It wasn't the gifts Khair waited for though, it was the time that they spent together that was most precious to her. Sometimes they'd stroll together in one of the smaller flower gardens at the back of the deorhi, other times they'd simply sit in Khair's bedroom and talk softly while they watched their son lie peacefully in his silver cradle. It was a beautiful cradle, finely engraved with intricate scroll patterns.

'Who does he look like?' James asked Khair one afternoon as they lay side-by-side in her huge carved bed. It was one of those languid afternoons when even the leaves on the trees outside seemed to be in a lazy mood. With no sign of a breeze, nothing was moving.

'Nobody I know.' Khair laughed in answer to James's question. 'What do you think, Eshgham?'

James propped himself on his elbow and peered over at the infant. After observing him carefully for a few minutes, he smiled and nodded. 'I think he looks like my father. He has many of his features and the expression on his face is a mirror image.'

'I have heard that he is very handsome. Is that true?' asked Khair with interest.

'Yes it is.' That of course was an understatement. James's father was in fact, commonly known as "The Handsome Colonel".[102] 'He is extraordinarily good looking. As is this little one,' added James then, glancing at his son.

'Well then, I am glad that he looks like him. Though I can see glimpses of myself in him too.'

'As long as he inherits some of your grace and good nature.' James looked at her lovingly. Yes, he'd fallen in love with her the instant he'd first seen her, but over the past few weeks, he'd witnessed a side to her, a softness, a tenderness, that he hadn't seen before. Sometimes he was even surprised at how involved a mother she was. Most women from aristocratic families did not bother themselves with trivial things, leaving the child-rearing completely to the nurses and nannies. Khair was different. With her gentle ways and loving nature, motherhood seemed to come naturally to

102 Heritage, Hollydale Open Space Website, U.K.

her[103] and James found himself falling more deeply in love with her than ever before. So much so, that his own helplessness at not being able to take her and the baby with him to live in the Residency, tore at his heart. They were supposed to be a family, after all. Yet, he hadn't even been able to tell his own brother the truth. On the contrary, he'd been lying about it to him. It was almost like living two different lives at the same time, one that he'd chosen for himself and the other that he was being compelled to live.

'What are you thinking?' She looked at him with concern and he couldn't help being astonished at her ability to read his mood so accurately every time.

'I was thinking about us,' he admitted to her then. They were always honest with each other. 'We are a family. We should be living together.' He shook his head wearily. 'Sometimes I cannot believe the way I have been rendered helpless. Is it really worth it? Is it?'

She knew he was talking about his job and she gently placed her hand over his. 'Of course it is worth it. So, we have to wait a while. We will wait. Inshallah, we will soon be together. You, me and him.' She glanced at the baby who was now staring animatedly up at the carved, gilded ornament on the side of the cradle. Usually when Khair was alone with the baby, a wet nurse sat by the side of the cradle, a velvet cushion on her lap for the baby to rest on. But when James visited them, they liked their privacy.

Now he nodded at her words and leaned his head back into the pillows. 'Inshallah!' he repeated after her. 'I hope you are right my darling Khair, for nothing would make me happier than to see the three of us living together, as a family should.'

---

103 Laslocky, Megan. *The Little Book of Heartbreak: Love gone wrong through the ages.* USA. Plume, a member of Penguin Group, USA. January, 2013.

'That will happen too, but rather than worry about the future, why cannot we rejoice in the present?' Khair smiled at her husband.

'Yes, you are correct. After all, "this moment is all there is", according to Rumi. That is, if you are familiar with his teachings,' James teased her with a twinkle in his eye. They both laughed then as they remembered the first time she'd quoted Rumi to him. It was heartening to know that other than deep love and respect for each other, they also shared the kind of camaraderie that allowed them to laugh together.

The first few weeks passed very quickly for them as Khair and the baby got into a daily routine. Khair kept herself busy reading books, getting regular massages, making bangles, taking long languid walks in the flower gardens and spending time with her new baby, and her days seemed to pass at an astonishing pace. She was admittedly astounded when James announced to her one day that the baby was already almost three months old. Time was certainly flying and even now it seemed as though the night of her sister's wedding when she'd seen him for the very first time from behind that tassled silk curtain, had only just happened.

They were already well into summer that year when news came from Calcutta; rather disturbing news. The Governor General had written to James, asking him to renegotiate the Subsidiary Treaty which had been signed only a few months back. Not surprisingly, the demands that he made and the changes that he wanted were blatantly unfair and unjust. In fact, even while he read the order, James couldn't help wondering whether other than his own greedy ambition, the Governor General also took some sort of pleasure in tormenting James with jobs that he knew James found morally impossible to carry out. After all, bullying, browbeating and using aggression to make the Nizam sign a treaty which would reduce him and the state of Hyderabad to mere subservience to the British, were against his principles and ethics. It was at times like these that he really did have to ask himself the inevitable questions. Was resigning from the post that he otherwise loved, that he'd worked so hard to attain, was it really the only viable option now? Would he really have to give up his dreams in order to protect his conscience? Was it going to ultimately be a choice between integrity and duty?

Unable to find the answers, James would then sit down and write to his friend, William Palmer, the Resident at the Pune durbar. Really, who could understand his predicament better than Palmer? After all, an Indian wife wasn't the only thing that Palmer and he had in common. In fact, like James, Palmer had also been at the receiving end of Wellesley's wrath. Palmer's candid love for India, his forthright manner, his contempt for the bigoted and prejudiced attitudes of some of his own countrymen, had made him unpopular with many in the Company. James knew that despite the fact that his brother and he had always shared a special bond, it was Palmer who had gone through the same difficulties as James and would likely understand his situation better than anyone else. In that sense, they were like kindred spirits, Palmer and he. With very similar value systems, a mutual respect had formed between the two men and James was grateful to have someone with whom he could express his thoughts without feeling judged.

It was however, only later that year that Wellesley took a final decision about Palmer. From Wellesley's point of view, Palmer had completely failed to align himself with Wellesley's vision, or deliver on what was expected of him as far as the Marathas were concerned.

Palmer of course knew the Marathas well, and he understood that the objectives being pursued by the Governor General were impossible to achieve. He had tried to communicate this to Wellesley in the past too, that the Marathas were a proud warrior race and would never willingly allow themselves to be subjugated or controlled by the British or anyone else. Wellesley did not see things that way and he had taken a decision to remove Palmer from the position of Resident of Pune.[104] This decision should not have astonished anyone. Palmer and Wellesley had never shared a camaraderie or even an understanding of any kind. Anyway, it was now clear that William Palmer's role as Resident of Pune was over, and it was time for him and his family to pack their belongings and set sail for Calcutta.

Travel to Calcutta via Hyderabad then. James found himself writing to Palmer in his next letter. *Come and stay with me for a few days. There is plenty of room for you and the Begum, as well as your entourage, here at the Residency. I assure you; we shall have a fine time. The forests hereabouts are excellent hunting grounds and the khansama is one of the best in the city.* He knew of course, that these were mere formalities because the truth was that both Palmer and he were going through a challenging phase and would be glad of an opportunity to offer comfort to each other. *It will be splendid to have a friend to speak with for a change,* added James then in his letter. *I must admit that I am rather tired of the hostility.* Palmer would understand what he was referring to. Other than the antagonism from Calcutta, James had also lately been facing problems from within the Subsidiary Force in Hyderabad. James's native ways were certainly a major reason

104 Fuhr, Enid M. Thesis on Strategy and Diplomacy in British India Under Marquis Wellesley. King's College, University of London, 1988.

for this, but news of his association with Khair had made things much worse.

He finished the letter to Palmer then and sealed it. It would be good to have him and his family stay at the Residency for a few days. And a major decision he'd taken recently would make things very comfortable for Palmer's *begum* too. With her gentle ways and graceful manner, James was certain that Khair would be an excellent hostess to his guests. He couldn't help smiling to himself as he recalled the excitement on her face when he'd finally brought her and little Ali to live with him at the Residency. Just seeing the pure joy in her eyes had touched his heart. Now they were a proper family at last. It really was high time.

15
Rang Mahal

James had thought that after living in her grandfather's deorhi for her entire life, Khair would take time to settle into her new home at the Residency zenana. He was pleasantly surprised when he saw the ease with which she made her way, not only into her new home, but also into the hearts of the people who lived there. Khair had a natural kindness and compassion about her, that made her instantly popular with everyone, from the ladies at the zenana to even the khansama in the Residency kitchen. Within a matter of a few weeks, she had managed to establish a routine for herself and Ali, and had also understood and acclimatized herself with the ways of the Residency. As for James, words could not have adequately described his happiness at finally having brought his wife and son home and he did everything he could to make the transition as smooth for them as he could. In fact, knowing that Khair had always lived very comfortably, James was getting a beautiful new zenana palace made for her. The construction had actually been underway for some time now, and James had been working tirelessly with his architect, poring over designs and plans and supervising the construction himself. It was going to be his gift to her, for he wanted to give his beloved wife the kind of home he knew she deserved. With a vast central courtyard, well-appointed bedrooms lavishly furnished in a splendid amalgamation of Palladian European and Mughal styles, an opulent dining area, charming *jharokhas* with breath-taking vistas of the estate and lush flower gardens[105] where Khair could spend the afternoons sipping tea or sherbet amidst the sounds of cooing pigeons and trickling fountains, the new zenana palace promised to be magnificent in every way.

'You will exhaust yourself, what with the new palace and everything else that is going on,' Khair told him one morning as they sipped tea in bed. It was actually already mid-morning but he'd been working late the previous night and she'd insisted that he sleep in. 'The doctor did tell you not to tire yourself out like this.' She was worried about him. He had started losing weight again and she didn't like the pallor of his face.

'The palace does not tire me, in fact, I take delight in it.' James looked at her affectionately and then sighed. Another autumn was already over and like the previous year, this one also seemed to have brought with it, new beginnings. Sometimes James couldn't help but wonder whether it was all actually the beginning to an end. So much seemed to be changing and the changes were happening at such a rapid pace that it was almost frightening at times. 'It is the other things that wear me out,' he continued. 'Sometimes I wonder why I even bother fighting them. It all seems utterly useless.'

Khair was distressed to hear her usually cheerful husband sounding so defeated. She understood politics and knew how brutal it could be. She knew that her husband was constantly living under a cloud of suspicion, that there were people in the Company who were convinced that he had switched sides and was in fact, a double

105 Interview and tour with Mr. S Anand, Registered Guide, Dept of Tourism, Govt of Telangana. January, 2022.

agent.[106] She was also aware of how much this pulled him down, how demoralizing it was for him.

'That investigation against me is being re-opened,' James informed her then. 'I suppose it was only a matter of time.'

'Yes, and now that we are living together, they have more reason than ever before to harass you.' She knew she sounded angry, furious even.

'Sometimes I feel as though it will haunt me forever.' James shook his head wearily. It had gone on for too long and he knew that this time too, his colleagues would be summoned and thoroughly interrogated to investigate every minute detail of his life. It was a feeling akin to opening the doors of his house, even those of his bedroom, to strangers for scrutiny. Like any man, he wanted to shield his family from the prying eyes of the world, but it seemed as though the more he tried, the more their private life was laid bare and open for everyone to see.

Turning toward his wife, he suddenly noticed the anxious expression on her face.

'Do not worry, my darling. Everything will be all right.' James placed his tea cup on the side table and leaned over to kiss her.

Lifting her face toward his, Khair's arms immediately went around him, drawing him closer. Even as he brought his lips down on hers and inhaled the scent of her body, James smiled to himself at how hopelessly attracted they still were to each other, despite being married for several months. Undoubtedly, their passion for each other was the same. He could hardly resist her when she looked at him like that, with her eyes full of invitation and longing.

---

106 Dr Subhadra Anand. Noted Historian. Documentary on 10 Love Stories. Epicon.

'You will make me very late,' he laughed then, pulling away from her. 'I have many things to do today. There is hardly any time left for the General and his begum to arrive. I have to start making preparations.'

'That is not a problem, Eshgham.' Khair moved closer to him again and rested her head on his shoulder. 'Leave it to me. I will get everything ready for them.'

'You have enough on your plate. With Ali and now this little one.' He placed a gentle hand on her rapidly swelling belly. On Khair's lithe body, the pregnancy had already started showing. 'I will ask Aziz Ullah to make all the necessary arrangements. He is very competent.'

'I hope their visit goes well, Inshallah.' Khair briefly closed her eyes and drew a deep breath. 'The General is a good man. I have never met him, but from everything you tell me, he seems to be a lot like you.'

'Yes, we are alike in more ways than one.' He kissed the top of her head and then threw off the soft muslin razai. Swinging his long legs over the four-poster bed, he slipped his feet into khussas[107] and then turned around to look at his wife. 'It is good we spoke about the Palmers' visit. I must remember to talk to Aziz Ulla today about getting their living arrangements organized. They will be here soon and I hear the begum travels with a very substantial entourage.'

Not surprisingly, the Palmers' visit proved to be a much-needed respite for James and Khair. The General and James had already developed a camaraderie through the letters they'd exchanged over

---

107 A kind of shoe, resembling slippers.

the years, but the friendship that formed between the two women was instant and spontaneous. The similarities in their backgrounds must have helped, but that was only one part of it. A strange, inexplicable bond seemed to immediately form between them, a kind of friendship that is rare and extraordinary. To anyone who saw them together, it was impossible to believe that they hadn't known each other all their lives. In fact, from the way that they instantaneously took to each other, it seemed as though each had found a soul sister in the other. While James and the General went hunting or played cards or billiards, the two ladies spent many happy hours in each other's company over the next few weeks. And it wasn't even just friendship, it was an unquestionable trust, a faith that they had in each other which allowed Khair to confide in the older woman, to talk to her about things that she hadn't discussed with anyone else. Undoubtedly, Faiz Baksh had quickly become Khair's closest friend and confidante.

One afternoon, they had taken their embroidery out to the garden in the compound beside the recently completed *Rang Mahal*, the magnificent zenana palace that James had built for Khair.[108] Khair had fallen in love with it the moment James had presented it to her upon completion, but everyone else who had seen it had confirmed that no Indian prince had as beautiful a zenana as this one. Even Faiz was visibly impressed the first time she saw it. The verdant gardens that surrounded it, the *kabutar khana* that had been especially constructed, the marble fountains spouting crystal clear water, the walls and ceilings resplendent with brilliant pictures of

108 Ali Khan, Raza. *Hyderabad 400 Years*. Hyderabad, India. Zenith Services. 1991.

birds, flowers and beasts,[109] it was truly the finest even she had seen and everyone knew that Faiz Baksh was a lady used to the very best.

'It certainly is magnificent. And the gardens are splendid,' she said now as she looked around at the vast expanse of fruit trees and flowering plants. They were sitting under the shaded canopy of three mango trees and in the distance, they could hear the cooing of pigeons.

'A sound that always has a calming effect on me,' remarked Khair blithely then. 'As it does on James.'

'He does seem to be very keen on gardening.' Faiz smiled at Khair. 'The General was telling me that he would like to add an English garden to the estate sometime.'

'Yes, and a Chinese garden as well.' Khair smiled back at her friend.

'It is a relaxing thing to do.' Faiz nodded approvingly. 'It will take his mind off other things. He has been troubled lately, no?'

'Well, he looked very calm today,' commented Khair. 'Being with the General is good for him.'

The men had gone into the forest for a day of hunting. Just like James, the General too enjoyed hunting which other than being a favourite sport, was also considered a show of masculinity.[110] Like most sahibs, James also always took along his entourage of horses, elephants, tame cheetahs, cooks, *hookahburdars* and of course, *shikaris* on his hunting expeditions. While the bond between these

---

109 Interview with and research paper by Dr Aruna Pariti on "British Residency", Department of History, Osmania Women's College (Former British Residency), Hyderabad, India. February, 2022.

110 Mani, Fiona. *Guns and Shikaris: The rise of the sahib's hunting ethos and the fall of the subaltern poacher in British India, 1750-1947.* Research Repository, West Virginia University, 2012.

indigenous hunters and the sahibs who depended on them, was certainly fascinating, it was the cheetahs who were truly intriguing. It was nothing less than astounding to see how easily these huge spotted cats could be tamed. 'Almost as gentle and loyal as dogs,' James often said. 'It is indeed delightful to see how much they enjoy being petted, even by strangers sometimes.' As always, today also he had taken his cheetahs with him on the expedition. They would spend the day in the wild, hunting jackals, bison and spotted deer, although the challenge of hunting the extraordinarily swift and nimble black buck was particularly thrilling. Later, canvas tents would be set up in the camp with the sahibs' tents always pitched in the most favourable location. Afterward, they would enjoy an evening of food, drink, hookah, music and dance. James always had the best dance girls performing, especially if he was entertaining a special friend like the General. The ladies didn't mind the absence of their husbands at all. They were perfectly happy to spend time with each other. Particularly on a beautiful winter afternoon like this.

'It is good for him to spend time with a friend like the General,' repeated Khair then as they watched the pigeons and parakeets flutter past in a gay display of myriad colours. 'I am so glad you came to stay.'

Faiz leaned over and gently placed her hand on the younger woman's shoulder. 'I know things have not been easy for you recently.'

'Are they ever?' Khair wondered aloud. 'After all, the decisions we have made, the paths we have chosen, are not going to be easy ones to tread. We always knew that.'

'They are good men,' remarked Faiz, referring to the General and James. 'Honest, straightforward and ethical. It is no wonder that Wellesley does not like them.'

'They would never fit into his policy. That is why he would like to get rid of them.' Khair shrugged. 'It is a matter of ethics. They could never agree with men like Wellesley, their conscience would not allow it.'

'Yes, and we are now paying the price for it.' Faiz smiled wryly. 'Perhaps you may want to ask James to be careful. I know his brother William is to replace the General at the Pune durbar, but with his health being the way it is....' She hesitated for a moment before completing her sentence. 'What I am trying to say is that it seems unlikely that William will be able to continue in the position for very long. We do not know who will ultimately take his place, but I am sure that he will not be one who James will see eye-to-eye with.'

'At least not if Wellesley has his way,' Khair agreed with her and then waved a delicate hand in the air. 'Let us change the subject. It is much too beautiful a day to be talking about Wellesley.'

They both laughed and Khair stretched her legs out on the marble *paidan*. She was already more than seven months pregnant and had been told to start taking it easy.

'Not too long to go now, is it? asked Faiz then, with a motherly look at the younger woman. 'You must not think too much. It is not good to worry at a time like this. You must have faith in him. He is a very capable man.'

Khair smiled at the obvious affection in Faiz's voice. 'I cannot help worrying about his health,' she confessed to her. 'The headaches, the stomach cramps, the muscle pain, it is becoming worse. *Ya Allah, yeh kambakht tehkikaat!* (O Lord, these damn investigations!) It has certainly taken a toll on him.'

'What does the doctor say?' Like James, the General may have gone native in many ways, but when it came to medical treatment, he too, like most British officers, relied on the English doctor who had treated him for years.[111]

Khair sighed. Talking about this was never easy, but strangely, she felt she could speak to Faiz about anything. A camaraderie, a solidarity, now existed between them. 'I know Dr Ure is concerned. He may not have said it in so many words, but I know he feels that if things do not improve, James might have to consider moving to England.'

Faiz shook her head. 'James would never do that. India is his home, just like it is for the General. He would never be able to live anywhere else.'

Khair nodded. 'You are right. This is the only home he knows. Although his brother William has already been advised to move back. As you know, his health has deteriorated recently and the doctor feels that the climate in England will be better for him.'

'Have you discussed it with James?'

'No, he will not even talk about it. He is too devoted to me and Ali. And now, with this little one on the way....' Khair smiled, trailing off.

'Inshallah, everything will be all right. Do not worry. Revel in his love. Look around you.' Faiz waved a hand in the direction of the new palace. 'He did this for you.'

'Yes, my beautiful Rang Mahal. For me, it is *Jannat* itself.' Khair put a hand to her heart. 'Every wall, every window, every room in here resonates with his love for me.'

---

111 Saini, Anu. *Physicians of Colonial India.* National Library of Medicine, India. July – Sept, 2016.

A maid appeared then, bearing a tray. On it was a silver surahi filled with rose and almond sherbet and two silver tumblers, along with a big platter of succulent kebabs.

Faiz placed her embroidery down on the wrought-iron garden table and rubbed her hands together. 'Ah! Khair's famed Residency Kebabs.[112] I have heard your recipe is unparalleled.'

Khair laughed. Her kebabs had become famous all over the city and were now popularly known as "Residency Kebabs".

'Enough talk, it is time for some indulgence now.' Faiz wagged a finger at Khair, feigning sternness. 'As for you, my dear, lunch was hours ago. That little one in there must be hungry.'

---

112 Interview with Salma Yusuf Hussain. Food Historian and Persian Scholar. May, 2022.

16
Noor-un-Nissa, Sahib Begum

Just like all good things, their time together seemed to come to an end far too quickly and before they knew it, the Palmers had to prepare to depart for Calcutta. Winter and early spring was a beautiful time in Hyderabad, and the weeks certainly seemed to have flown. So much so, that they had come to think of each other as family rather than just friends, and not surprisingly, all of them looked sad when the day finally arrived for them to leave.

'I am going to miss you so much.' Faiz had tears in her eyes as they stood on the portico of the bungalow, minutes before their departure. 'You must come and visit us as soon as you can,' she insisted then, even as Khair nodded and smiled.

'I have never gone anywhere beyond Hyderabad. But I will come and visit you. I just wish you could have stayed on a little longer.'

'I wish we could too. Particularly since the joyous occasion is just days away.' Faiz placed a gentle hand on Khair's belly. 'Any time now, I would say. Please take good care of yourself, my dear Khair.'

'I will.' Khair pressed the box she was holding into Faiz's hands. 'I made these for you. I hope you will wear them and remember me.'

Faiz opened the box. Resting on the downy velvet lining were two dozen, beautifully embellished, enamel bangles. During her stay in Hyderabad, Faiz had admired Khair's flair for designing jewellery, but these were truly spectacular. It was evident that Khair had worked very hard on them.

'They are beautiful.' Faiz stepped forward and took the younger woman in her arms. 'You are precious to me. Take care of yourself and of James too,' she repeated then. 'I am sure we will meet very soon. Very soon indeed.'

The General who was standing on the side with James, glanced at his pocket watch. 'We must be on our way now,' he reminded his wife with a gentle smile. 'It is getting late.'

Faiz wiped her eyes with her handkerchief. 'Do not forget to write to me as soon as the little one makes an appearance. I am to be the Godmother, am I not?'

'Who else would be?'

The two women hugged one last time and then the Palmers finally got into the waiting palanquins. They were to travel by road to Masulipatam, from where they would take a fast boat on to Calcutta. It was going to be a long journey.

As it turned out, Faiz had been right about the baby. Soon after the Palmers had departed from Hyderabad, on 9 April, 1802[113], Khair went into labour. Like the previous time, it was a beautiful spring day and Khair had an uneventful delivery with her mother and husband by her side. This time, she gave birth in her beloved Rang Mahal. Once all the rituals had been completed, they named the little girl Noor-un-Nissa, light among women. Then once again, as he had done for his son, James went on to add a title to his newborn's name. Noor-un-Nissa, *Sahib Begum.* James and Khair were now the proud parents of two beautiful children.

---

113 Katherine Aurora Winsloe (Kirkpatrick). Noor-un-Nissa. Sahib Begum. Geni. Genealogy.

Just like the days that had followed their son's birth, James and Khair once again revelled in the joys of parenthood. They spent many happy hours together every day, playing with their children in the gardens of the Residency. James had recently invited his mother-in-law to live with them at the Residency and between two loving parents and a doting grandmother, not to mention a fleet of nannies and nurses, the children were extremely loved and well looked after. James was a devoted and attentive parent to both of them, as was Khair. Unlike many of the other aristocratic women, Khair was much too emotional to leave her children completely to the nannies and nurses. She spent a lot of time with them, and once her confinement period was over, she often took them to visit friends and relatives in the palaces around the city. They frequently stopped over at Aristu Jah's zenana, with whom they had excellent relations, and Ali and Noor would play there happily with the other children. Like the others, Ali and Noor were being brought up as Muslims with Persian being spoken around them all the time. Even though James did get clothes and toys sent over from England for his children to familiarize them with English dress and look, their upbringing was predominantly Hyderabadi. Of course, once they were older, aristocratic Muslim children were taught by private tutors and this was usually commemorated by a ceremony called *bismillah* which would mark the start of education. Ali and Noor, however, would eventually be sent to England to study, as was the case with most children from mixed marriages. Khair and James, though aware of this, didn't talk about it very often. The children were still young and there was time.

'How fast they seem to grow,' Khair commented to James one day as they watched Ali play with a set of painted toy soldiers that had come in from England, while his sister watched him contentedly from her cradle. Young though they were, it already seemed as if a deep bond existed between the siblings.

'Look at him, trying hard to walk on his own.' James laughed, watching his son. He had found his feet recently and could easily stand up by himself.

'He is trying to impress his sister,' said Khair then. 'It is adorable, the way he dotes on her.' Ali had also lately been experimenting with words, mostly Persian. He was a happy child with a sunny disposition and an easy smile. With his pale complexion, light hair and Anglo-Saxon features, he was growing up to look more than ever like his paternal grandfather.

'It is a good thing that both the children have such fair skin colour.' Khair smiled at James. 'It will be easier for them when they go to England.'

Surprised, James turned to look at his wife. This was the first time she'd spoken so candidly about the inevitable separation that lay ahead for them. Even though it had been unsaid until now, both of them knew that the children would eventually have to go to England. Not all Anglo-Indian children were sent, though.[114] James and Khair were also not unaware about the prejudices that children of mixed race faced, particularly those with darker skin colour. Skin colour was such an important factor when it came to acceptance from their British families. Everyone knew that children with paler complexions were more easily accepted than their darker counterparts, who on several occasions, were even disowned by their British relatives. In fact, siblings were often even separated on the basis of skin colour, with the fairer ones being packed off to

114 Interview with Rana Safvi. Historian and Writer. May, 2022.

England to study and live with their British families, and the darker ones being made to stay back in India.[115] Those who "passed off" as English were easily accepted into the social fabric there and later even went on to attain high office.

'Well, I am just glad that they have both inherited your easy disposition.' James slipped an arm around Khair. 'Look at Noor. Never cranky, always ready with a big smile for us.'

As though perfectly on cue, the infant suddenly flashed a toothless grin at her parents and they both laughed.

'I am actually surprised you even brought it up,' said James. 'If I remember correctly, you always prefer to turn to procrastination and denial in situations that you do not like.' There was an affectionate look in his eyes as he teased her, but Khair shook her head.

'I am a mother now. I have to be brave and learn to accept difficult situations.'

'Difficult situations!' James smiled wryly at her words. 'They seem to have besieged us from the very beginning, have they not? I hope they will soon be over. Or at least I hope we get a reprieve from them.'

Almost as though it had been a moment of wish fulfilment, not long after, news arrived for James and Khair, much awaited news. The investigation against James which had once again been well underway for several months, was finally being closed. This time though, it was not Sharaf-un-Nissa, but James's brother William, who had come to his rescue.[116] With his own health rapidly

115 Garcha, Ciara. The Curious Case of Kitty Kirkpatrick. Our Shared Cultural Heritage. 4 August 2020.

116 Chancey, Marla Karen. *In the Company's Secret Service.* Thesis. Florida State University Library. 2003.

deteriorating, William could no longer refute the fact that his time in India was over. The doctor had told him in no uncertain terms that if he wished to even partially recover his health, he had to bid goodbye to India and move to England. With his own career clearly over, William had decided to try and salvage his brother's career instead and had written to Wellesley, taking the entire blame for the concealment of the affair between James and Khair. With William now taking responsibility, Wellesley had no option but to acquit James of all charges. After all, in every other respect, James had been an able officer and a wonderful diplomat. And so, the investigation that had caused unimaginable anguish and torment to James and taken a toll on his state of mind and health over the years, was finally dropped. And though James was naturally, immensely relieved at the turn of events, he was admittedly also weary, exhausted and fed up of the incessant worrying. He now wanted to leave it all behind and focus his entire attention on his home and family. He wanted to spend time with his wife and children and get the main Residency building renovated. The gardens needed improvement, new rooms needed to be added and there were entire sections of the building that were beyond repair and would have to be torn down and rebuilt. And so, despite knowing what the outcome would be, James once again applied to Calcutta for funds to remodel.

'Do you suppose he will grant the funds?' Aziz Ullah asked him one day, looking doubtful. 'I do not suppose he is very pleased about having to close the investigation so unceremoniously.'

'No, he is not pleased.' James agreed with his munshi. 'He would much rather have preferred to see me removed from my position and subsequently punished for the grave offences I have committed.'

Aziz Ullah looked distressed at James's weary tone. 'Has there been any news from Pune?' he asked then. Sir Barry Close had been appointed as the new Resident at Pune. James knew that Wellesley was very fond of Close and considered him one of his best men.[117]

James shook his head. 'Not really. After all, Colonel Barry Close is not like my good friend, Palmer. I do not think he is comfortable discussing any developments with me. Perhaps like the Wellesley brothers, Close also thinks I am a traitor and not to be trusted.' Leaning back into his chair, James closed his eyes, as though overcome with exhaustion.

'You have tormented yourself enough Sahib.' Aziz Ullah's tone was gentle. 'Do not worry anymore. I am sure the funds will not be sanctioned from Calcutta, but I am also equally certain that another better solution will present itself.'

James opened his eyes and looked gratefully at his old munshi. What a wonderful support he had been to him over the years![118]

'You are right Aziz,' he agreed then. 'We must think of an alternative plan if Calcutta does not sanction the funds for the renovation.'

'It might be a good idea to speak to the Nizam, Sahib. He might be able to help. Perhaps you could discuss it with the Prime Minister first? He is very fond of you.'

James's face broke into a smile. Rising from his chair, he came around the desk and patted his munshi on the back. 'You do have good ideas Aziz. Solomon might indeed be able to help me. I have

---

117 Fuhr, Enid M. *Thesis on Strategy and Diplomacy in British India Under Marquis Wellesley*. King's College, University of London, 1988.

118 Wilkinson, Callie. *Relationships between the Political Residents of the English East India Company and their munshis, 1798-1818.* Wolfson College, University of Cambridge.

three excellent roundheads that have just come in from England. I hear he has expanded the size of his pit and the roundheads will make a fine present. Please schedule a meeting with him.'

17
James's Dream

The Nizam's family owned several grand palaces in the city. Built by Nizam Salabat Jung and situated just a few kilometres from the Charminar, it was however the Chowmahalla Palace which was the seat of the Asaf Jahi Dynasty and the official residence of the Nizam.[119] With its massive palace grounds, enormous courtyards and sprawling gardens, the complex actually housed four different palaces in four directions, making the name Chowmahalla perfectly appropriate.

The architecture of the palace, much like many of the palaces in Hyderabad, was a unique amalgamation of several architectural styles and influences. James had visited the Chowmahalla Palace innumerable times, yet it was the sheer grandeur of it that never ceased to amaze him. The majestic durbar hall where the Nizam would assemble with his ministers, the *Takht-e-Nishan* or the royal seat, the clock tower with the Khilwat clock, the Corinthian columns, the intricate stucco work on the roof, the fountains, the oil portraits on the walls.[120] It was all in simple words, overwhelmingly

---

119 Stewart, Stanley. India's Sleeping Beauty Awakes. *The Times*, UK. 28 November 2010.

120 Interview and tour with Mr. S Anand, Registered Guide, Dept of Tourism, Govt of Telangana. January, 2022.

magnificent. 'Suffice it to say that thirty-eight people are employed just to dust the many Belgian chandeliers that adorn the ceilings of the sprawling, gilded durbar hall,' James often remarked to visitors, the admiration palpable in his voice. 'The moment you ascend that flight of stone steps at the entrance, you will feel as though you are entering a different world.'

His purpose of visiting the palace this time was a very special one. After the expected response had come in from Calcutta, denying the request for funds, James had discussed the matter with Aristu Jah. Having gone through so much together, the relationship between him and the Prime Minister had only become stronger and they had discussed the matter of the reconstruction quite candidly. On the Prime Minister's advice, James had then taken the reconstruction proposal to the Nizam, who on seeing the sheer magnitude of the plan, had declined it too.[121] His refusal though, had been much gentler, compared to the curt response that had come in from the Governor General. 'The plan does indeed look a little intimidating. I suppose he thinks you are trying to stake your claim on huge areas of land,' Aristu Jah had teased James, a twinkle in his eye. Then he added thoughtfully. 'Perhaps you could have it drawn on a smaller map? That might do the trick.' It sounded like a sensible suggestion to James, certainly worth trying. After all, what did he have to lose? He immediately had the architect design the plan again and then scheduled another visit to the palace.

Having been a regular guest at the palace had made James adept at the process followed by visitors. On entering, the purpose of the

---

121 Interview with and research paper by Dr Aruna Pariti on "British Residency", Department of History, Osmania Women's College (Former British Residency), Hyderabad, India. February, 2022.

visit was first written on a piece of paper and then a gold coin was placed in a box. This was followed by a brief wait in one of the resting rooms before permission was granted to meet with the Nizam. The palace had two entrances, the western entrance was reserved for the Nizam and the northern entrance for everyone else.[122] That day also, James entered the palace from the northern side. The detailed plan of the proposed Residency drawn on a smaller map as per the Prime Minister's advice, was tucked safely under one arm. In his other hand, he carried presents for his old friend; a gold necklace encrusted with pearls and rubies, a soft downy fur coat and a pair of acrobatic pigeons. Even as he waited for the Nizam to summon him, James acknowledged to himself that his mood was optimistic. Aristu Jah knew the Nizam very well and if he thought that he would be more receptive to the same plan drawn on a smaller map, then James wanted to believe that the Prime Minister was right.

Two hours later, he re-emerged from the palace, a smile playing on his lips. Not only had the Nizam approved the funds for the reconstruction, he had also granted him ownership of the fields around the Residency.[123] Just thinking about it, made James want to start the project right away. Afterward, the older gentleman had even become a little emotional. James had offered a nazar which had been accepted with a smile. The Nizam had then embraced James warmly, but James had noticed that his old friend wasn't looking particularly well that day. Age certainly seemed to be taking its toll and he'd been looking frailer of late. In fact, people who had seen the

122 Interview and tour with Mr. S Anand, Registered Guide, Dept of Tourism, Govt of Telangana. January, 2022.

123 Interview with and research paper by Dr Aruna Pariti on "British Residency", Department of History, Osmania Women's College (Former British Residency), Hyderabad, India. February, 2022.

Nizam in his youth, could hardly believe that the toothless, sixty-eight-year-old seated on the *musnud*[124], was the same forbidding and ruthless man they had once known. He seemed more and more like a shadow of his former self these days.

In any case, now was not the time to think disheartening thoughts. The Nizam had agreed to finance the renovation project and that was a major relief to James. So much so, that he couldn't wait to set up a meeting with his team of architects and start planning. James was not unaware of the fact that a project of such enormous scale and proportions would take every ounce of energy and time from those involved in it. To say that the work was humungous would be an understatement. Designs would have to be drawn up and then the best masons, bricklayers, carpenters and painters in the city would be hired before construction could officially start. Admittedly, James had a dream. He wanted the British Residency which had been built by his brother, the home where Khair and he had given birth to their dreams, where he had spent the happiest, most memorable days of his life with his wife and children, to be the epitome of grandeur and opulence, admired and hailed by everyone who saw it. It wouldn't just be a building, no, it would be an icon, an embodiment of his desires, his hopes, his wishes. No visitor to Hyderabad would leave without visiting it at least once. They would see it and then they would marvel at its beauty, its splendour. They would go back and talk about it, for years and decades and perhaps even centuries. It was a spectacular dream, but James was willing to work as hard as he needed to, to turn it into a beautiful reality.

The next few weeks were fraught with activity at the Residency. With the work scheduled to begin shortly, James's hands were full.

---

124 A cushioned seat used as a throne by princes of India.

His focus was now firmly on the construction project and he was constantly busy with the team of architects. When he had the time though, James devoted himself completely to his family. He would spend hours with Ali and little Noor, regaling them with fascinating tales from his own childhood, including the years he had spent in Eton as a boy. While he wanted them to know about English ways and traditions, after all, that was a part of their heritage too, the bigger reason was to familiarize them so that it did not feel like a completely alien culture to them when they went there for their education. Other times, he played simple games with them or took them for long walks around the property as he introduced them to the wide variety of plants, trees and flowers. 'You must embrace new skills and techniques when it comes to gardening,' he explained to them one day. 'But never abandon the age-old practices that have stood the tests of time.' Smiling down at them, he then repeated to his children what their mother often said. 'A well laid out garden is a place of rest, of reflection. Akin to paradise or jannat.' James knew that in Persian life, gardens are a symbol of happiness and prosperity.[125] In fact, according to the Koran, the garden is used as an earthly analogue for life in paradise. Islamic gardens focused greatly on the sensory experience, hence the wider use of water and aromatic plants in Islamic gardens. Unlike English gardens, which were usually designed for walking, an Islamic garden was a place for rest and contemplation. Now with the reconstruction, their home would have both. The Hindoostani garden in the compound beside Rang Mahal was spectacular and James had also approved the plan for a complete English garden with extensive parklands, a Chinese

125 Interview with Mr. M.A. Qayyum, Historian and Former Deputy Director, Department of Archaeology and Museums, Hyderabad. March, 2022.

garden where a wide variety of medicinal herbs would be grown, and a variety of fruit orchards.

With plans and ideas for the new Residency firmly in place, it seemed as though once again a new autumn was heralding in a fresh start. After much deliberation and thought, James had hired Lt Samuel Russell of the Madras Engineers for designing and supervising the job.[126] A brilliant man, Russell designed the building in the Palladian style of architecture and ironically, the plans bore a striking resemblance to Wellesley's own Governor House in Calcutta.[127] James couldn't help smiling when he thought about Wellesley's reaction to that, particularly since he had refused the grant of funds for the project himself. He said as much to Aziz Ullah one day, as they sat in James's study, poring over the plans.

'Pardon me for saying this Sahib, but I hear that the Governor House is also modelled after the famous St. Petersburg Palace in Russia,' said Aziz Ullah then.

James laughed. 'Yes, that is what I understand. Some people even believe that it is modelled after Kedleston Hall in Derbyshire. Anyway, I suppose it is better that the project is being financed by the Nizam. The Governor General would never have approved a project of this scale.'

'It is going to be one of the most opulent buildings ever constructed in Hyderabad, Sahib.' Aziz Ullah pointed to the designs on James's desk in awe. 'Perhaps even in the whole of the Deccan.'

---

126 The Residency. Online Gallery. British Library.

127 Interview with and research paper by Dr Aruna Pariti on "British Residency", Department of History, Osmania Women's College (Former British Residency), Hyderabad, India. February, 2022.

James knew the old munshi was right as he glanced at the designs that Samuel Russell had finalized. The entrance to the building was going to be through a large pedimented portico, in the Neoclassical style. The portico, a staggering sixty feet in length, would have within its tympanum, the East India Company's Coat of Arms and the columns of the building would be in the slender ancient Greek Corinthian style. The portico would then lead into a hall of the same length and height. At each end would be oval rooms, including a dining room, a library and a drawing room, and at the corners would be smaller square rooms including a billiards room and an office. The semi-circular stairs in the centre would lead to the upper floor which would be a replica of the ground floor, uniformly carpeted, glazed and furnished with handsome, elegant English furniture. The building was to have three entrances, including one from the Musi River on the Southern side.[128] The entire building would be flanked on all sides by orchards, water bodies and gardens filled with the most exotic Indian, European and Chinese trees and plants, as well as a huge vegetable garden.

'A vegetable garden is a good idea, Sahib.' Aziz Ullah nodded approvingly at the mention of it. 'Would you like me to speak to the gardeners about ordering the seeds and other supplies? Is there anything special you would like?'

James leaned back in his chair and shook his head. 'Not really. As long as we can grow our own potatoes somehow. They really have become scarce, far too hard to come by.'

---

128 Interview with and research paper by Dr Aruna Pariti on "British Residency", Department of History, Osmania Women's College (Former British Residency), Hyderabad, India. February, 2022.

They both laughed and then the old munshi got up to go. There was too much work these days to sit around and spend their time in banter. No sooner had he left than James too put his paperwork away. It had been a long day and he wanted to head back to his family. These days, he just couldn't wait to get back to them. Ali was now running around everywhere and Noor had started babbling indiscernible little sounds that were like music to her adoring parents' ears. It seemed to James as though they had both grown a little more when he returned to them each evening. Watching them grow and flourish was a source of pure joy for him. Just like it would be with the renovation project. After all, James already knew that it was going to be nothing less than a marvellous piece of art once it was completed.

'Inshallah, at least for now, everything seems to be going well,' he smiled to himself then as he rose from the chair. 'I might as well make the best of my good fortune while it lasts. It certainly will not forever.'

18
Succession and Aggression

As it was every year, the summer of 1803 had been a hot one in Hyderabad. Thankfully, the heat hadn't slowed down the pace of work at the Residency. The estate in fact, had been throbbing with activity for weeks now, as hundreds of bricklayers, masons, carpenters and painters worked the hours away. For James and Khair, seeing their home being transformed into a thing of such sublime beauty was like a dream. So much so, that it was going to be very difficult to wait now. The grand durbar hall for which James had already ordered an enormous carpet measuring 60 feet by 30 feet, the glittering chandeliers including one that had been sold to the Company by the Prince of Wales,[129] the magnificent portico to the north and verandah to the south, the private apartments, the frescoed walls, the grand salon – they just couldn't wait to see it in all its splendour. As for Ali and Noor, they had been thrilled at the chaotic atmosphere, as children always are, and spent hours every day, watching the artisans at work. They never got in the way though, nor did they cause any trouble. Their cheerful, shy dispositions and easy smiles actually made them instantly popular

129 Finn, Margot and Smith, Kate. *The Russells in India: Anglo Indian Tastes. East India Company at Home, 1757-1857.* UCL Press.

with everyone and nobody minded when they came down to the grounds to watch the construction in progress.

James was lying in bed, listening to the sounds of the construction from his bedroom window one afternoon. The summer was almost over and the progress of the building had been incredible. His health though seemed to have deteriorated at an equally incredible pace. The painful rheumatism that he'd been living with for years, had reached almost unbearable levels recently. The flare-ups which had been rare months ago, had now become agonizingly common and there were days when he couldn't get out of bed at all. Sometimes even lifting a glass of water sent excruciating waves of agony down his arm and shoulder. And it wasn't just the rheumatism. He'd lost weight again and recently the episodes of abdominal pain had also increased. The fever came and went more frequently as did the nausea and loss of appetite. Dr Ure had been suspecting hepatitis for a while now. A particularly bad episode recently had confined him to bed for several days and even though she didn't always say it, James could sense Khair's constant anxiety and worry for him as she fussed around him, begging him not to push himself too much. Dr Ure though had been more candid with him, insisting that moving to England wasn't something he could dismiss any longer. 'It may not be a matter of choice anymore,' he'd said on his last visit. 'You cannot deny the fact that it might be your only option.'

Now as he struggled to a sitting position and watched the steady progress on the beautiful home he had envisioned, his children in the distance observing the workmen with rapt fascination, his lovely wife sitting peacefully in her sheesham chair with her embroidery, it was difficult to imagine that anywhere other than this, was his home. 'Why are things that we love the most always wrenched away so cruelly from us?' he wondered to himself then. 'Oh, if only my body would cooperate with me! Just thinking about leaving India, leaving my beloved country, shatters my heart. How would I ever survive that?' Heart-breaking though the thought was, deep down James knew that Dr Ure was right. Things that he had never imagined before, were now rapidly becoming very real possibilities. So real that for the first time in his thirty-nine years, he started thinking seriously about making out a will.

As a matter of fact, James was not the only one with health problems that summer. The Nizam, now aged sixty-nine, already had a history of heart trouble and the two strokes he'd suffered in 1801 had taken their toll. He'd had another stroke recently, which turned out to be the last straw, leaving the already ailing man in an exceedingly frail condition. Despite being well aware of the old man's deteriorating health for months, even James was genuinely shocked when he saw how gaunt and shrunken he looked after the stroke. It was almost as though the heart attack had sucked the last of his life out, and deeply saddening though it was to many, nobody was astonished when he finally breathed his last on 6 August that year.[130] Mir Nizam Ali Khan Siddiqi, Asaf Jah II, fourth son of Nizam-ul-Mulk, Asaf Jah I and Umda Begum, and second Nizam of Hyderabad, died peacefully in his sleep in the Chowmahalla Palace that had always been his home. The news spread like wildfire around Hyderabad, understandably causing immense apprehension and dread about the future of the city among its inhabitants. The Nizam had ruled the Deccan for more than four decades. He had been a liberal and kind

130 Ali Khan, Raza. *Hyderabad 400 Years.* Hyderabad, India. Zenith Services. 1991.

ruler, treating his subjects with compassion over the forty-two years that he had ruled. One of the most significant things he had done was to keep external and internal interferences at bay and maintain the autonomy of his state. He had settled issues of importance with the Marathas, entered into strategic treaties and organized administrative matters in Hyderabad.[131] A true connoisseur of the arts, under his rule, painters, dancers, musicians, poets and writers had blossomed. He had built gardens around the city, encouraged development and included women in matters of policy. 'He even bestowed Chanda Bibi with the rank of an *omrah* and gave her the formal title "Mah Laqa Bai" during one of the court celebrations last year,'[132] remarked James sadly to Khair. 'He was truly generous and progressive.'

James was correct in thinking that. There was so much good the Nizam had done for the city. Who would now take his place? Would the state of affairs in Hyderabad stay the same? Would the succession be a peaceful one? But even though the same questions plagued James's mind as they did everyone else's, the Nizam's death had also affected him in another way, a deeply personal one. The practical questions, the obvious misgivings, the inevitable policy changes notwithstanding, James had lost a dear friend, a father figure who had truly treated him like a beloved son.

Nizam Ali Khan was buried in the great marble courtyard of the Mecca Masjid, by the side of his mother Umda Begum.[133] It was

131 Pandharipande, Reeti and Nadimpally, Lasya. *A Brief History of the Nizams of Hyderabad.* Outlook Traveller. 5 August 2017.

132 Stewart, Courtney, A. *Feminine Power of the Deccan.* The Metropolitan Museum of Art, New York. Dept of Islamic Art.

133 Ali Khan, Raza. *Hyderabad 400 Years.* Hyderabad, India. Zenith Services. 1991.

indeed a sad day for Hyderabad for the city had lost a compassionate and tolerant ruler, but it became clear within days that the succession of his son, Sikander Jah, to the throne, was not going to be a particularly complex process. Sikander Jah was the Nizam's second son with his wife Tahniat un-nisa Begum, but most people were well aware of the fact that the new Nizam had inherited none of his father's good countenance or generosity of spirit. Given to self-indulgence and despondency, Sikander Jah was known to be brooding and suspicious by nature. He was not fully literate, could not even write or read Persian properly and spent far too much time in the company of women and wine.[134] There were even some who believed that the new Nizam actually suffered from an insanity of some sort. In any case, he had inherited a very prosperous state. What he did with it, still remained to be seen. James was still too pre-occupied juggling between the grief of losing his beloved friend and the relief that the succession had been a peaceful one, to think too much about the future just yet. Grieving peacefully though can also be a luxury, as James realized not long after. For within hours of the Nizam's death, Lord Wellesley wrote to the two major chieftains of the Maratha confederacy, Daulat Rao Sindhia and Raghoji Bhonsle II of Berar, declaring war on the Marathas. After the first war of 1775, which had continued into seven long years, this was the second major conflict between the East India Company and the Marathas.

This major decision, which would later go on to determine the strength and position of the British in India, was hardly an impulsive choice. At that time, the Maratha Empire comprised of five major

---

134 Dadabhoy, Bakhtiar K. *The Magnificent Diwan: The Life and Times of Sir Salar Jung 1.* India. Penguin Random House. 13 December 2019.

chieftains. These included the Peshwa in Pune, the Gaekwad chief of Baroda, the Sindhia chief of Gwalior, the Holkar chief of Indore and the Bhonsle chief of Nagpur. In October 1802, Peshwa Baji Rao II was defeated by Yashwantrao Holkar at The Battle of Poona. Baji Rao subsequently took British protection and signed the Treaty of Bassein with the Company. According to the treaty, the Peshwa could not enter into any treaty without consulting the British, could not declare war without British approval, would have to give up Surat and Baroda and could not even conduct his foreign affairs without British intervention. Furthermore, a British force of 6,000 troops would be permanently stationed with the Peshwa and any territorial claims made by him would be subject to arbitration by the Company.

This did not go down well with the other Maratha chieftains. There may have been internal issues between them, but they also shared something extremely significant with each other and that was a united sense of Maratha pride. Understandably, not only were they disgusted with the Peshwa for signing something so humiliating, they were also furious with the British. After supporting the Peshwa Raghunath Rao in 1775, now they had done the same with his son Baji Rao II. It was an insult to the honour of the Marathas and all the provocation they needed to unite against a common enemy. The Sindhia and Bhonsle rulers in particular, contested this treaty and later proved to be the biggest adversaries to it.

Now united in huge numbers, the efforts of the Marathas became bolder and more aggressive by the beginning of June 1803, and a new phase started between the British East India Company and the Marathas. There were two major events which led to this. The first was the march northwards from Poona on 4 June of the detachment of the company troops commanded by Arthur Wellesley. The second was the assembly near Malakpur of the armies of Daulat Rao Sindhia and Raja of Berar. In military terms, this could be considered a confrontation of the Company army and that of the Maratha confederacy. In diplomatic terms though, it was a clear contest between the East India Company and Sindhia for over lordship of the Peshwa.[135]

By early August, Arthur Wellesley had managed to take over the city of Ahmednagar. Information was subsequently received about the location of the Maratha army which was under the command of Colonel Anthony Pohlmann, a German formerly in British service. Wellesley's forces then moved towards the small village of Assaye, in pursuit of the Maratha cavalry-based army. When the British got there, though, they were greeted by a formidable sight. Sindhia's army was waiting for them, a sprawling force of fighters, well positioned behind the shallow Kailna river. Despite being outnumbered, Wellesley decided to move forward with the attack. Knowing that a frontal attack would have been perilous, his army snuck up to the enemy from the left, but the Maratha army was clearly ready for this. Both sides suffered enormous losses in the ensuing battle. Sindhia's modern infantry and impressive arrays of cannons were a match for Wellesley's men, who in turn, also used a smart combination of bayonet and cavalry charges, ultimately compelling the Marathas to retreat. By September 1803, not only had the Marathas lost to Wellesley's army at Assaye, they were also defeated by Lord Gerard Lake in Delhi. In November, Lake defeated

---

135 Bennell, A.S., The Anglo Maratha Confrontation of June and July 1803, *The Journal of the Royal Asiatic Society of Great Britain and Ireland.* Published by Cambridge University Press. Oct, 1962.

another Sindhia force at Laswari and Wellesley won over Bhonsle's forces at Argaon. It was evident though, that the British victory had come at an enormous cost.[136] The Marathas had lost, but what remained of the British army had also returned in an exhausted and battered state.

The fact that the Governor General had not accurately predicted the Maratha reaction, was actually strange. After all, he had spent several years in India and should have known what drove the local forces. He had not considered this outcome, nor had he sought the advice of those who had a sound understanding of the situation. He had instead, indulged his own ego and pride and caused a lot of needless bloodshed. The Britishers had indeed won, but the enormity of the loss of resources and life that the Company had suffered, was staggering. The victory had come at a very high cost as was also reiterated by one of Richard Wellesley's senior officers later. Wellesley's aggressive politics and insistence to subjugate and supress India had led to a terrible bloodbath, where along with the innumerable lives that had been lost, the image of the Company had also been tarnished. And this fact had not gone unnoticed by the Company's Board of Directors in London.

136 Ramanathan, Aditya. Battle of Assaye. *The Wire*. September, 2016.

19
End or the Beginning

'Like father, like son? Most certainly does not apply in this case.' James smiled wryly at his assistant and private secretary, Henry Russell. The two were usually honest with each other and James found it easy to share his mind with Russell, just like he did with Aziz Ullah.

'I agree.' Russell looked thoughtful. 'This one is different.'

They were talking about the new Nizam. Well, he wasn't actually new any longer. It was already almost nine months since he had succeeded his father to the throne. The succession had been a seamless one and had even been ratified by the Mughal emperor Shah Alam II.[137] James had attended the succession ceremony, but with a heavy heart. The Durbar Hall of the Chowmahalla Palace had been full of male guests who'd sat on a white cloth on the marble floor, while the women watched from the gallery upstairs. Sikander's family had been seated to the right of the throne. Then prayers in Arabic were chanted, followed by an inspection of the palace troops by the new Nizam. He'd entered the Durbar Hall, holding a gilded sword in his hand while verses from the Koran were recited. When he finally took his place on the throne, the ceremonial twenty-one-

---

137 Pandharipande, Reeti and Nadimpally, Lasya. A Brief History of the Nizams of Hyderabad. *Outlook Traveller*. 5 August 2017.

gun salute was followed by a chorus of "Long live the Nizam" from the throngs of people waiting out in the streets. For James, just seeing anyone other than his old friend seated on the musnud, had been heart-breaking.

'My primary responsibility as Resident of Hyderabad has always been to maintain cordial relations between the Nizam's durbar and the Company,' remarked James to Russell then. 'For the past nine months, this has not been an easy task.' And it wasn't just James. The general consensus was that Sikander Jah was as unlike his father as any son could be. Where the Nizam had been balanced and compassionate, Sikander's erratic and insensitive behaviour had recently shocked people. He thought nothing of remaining absent from the durbar for days, preferring to remain in total isolation instead. Most of the time, he did not even bother to meet with his ministers, or his family members.

'He has a naturally suspicious nature,' said Russell. 'But that is hardly surprising, considering the amount of time he spends with those personal attendants. All they do, all day, is to tell him stories about how deceitful and treacherous everyone is.'

James sighed. 'If only my old friend was here.' Russell knew he was referring to the late Nizam. 'How much I miss him, Russell! I hardly feel like visiting the durbar now.'

'How have the stomach ailments been treating you, sir?' Russell looked concerned. The health problems and then the shifting dynamics in Hyderabad's political scenario had taken a heavy toll on James. He just didn't look like himself these days.

'It has not been good,' confessed James. 'It has not been an easy time. The passing of the Nizam, the problems from Calcutta, my own health – it has just been one thing after another. As they say, "When sorrows come, they come not single spies, but in battalions."

It was not very long after that James understood the full enormity of his own words. If he had thought things were difficult before, he should have waited a while. For in the first week of May that year, news came from Aristu Jah's palace that the Prime Minister had been taken ill. James's first reaction to this was astonishment. A strapping, indomitable presence in the durbar and wherever else he went, Aristu Jah had never complained of any major health problems. He had on the contrary, always been in robust health. The fact that he had fallen sick was bewildering. 'Though of course, a fever can inflict anyone,' James commented to Khair the next day, trying to maintain an optimistic approach. 'I am sure dear Solomon will recover very soon.'

'Inshallah!' Khair cupped her hands and joined them by the sides in the traditional Islamic gesture. Aristu Jah had accepted her as his daughter, even given her a share from his jagir. The two families had enjoyed a long and strong friendship for many years, and Khair was very fond of him. She had been visibly distressed ever since she'd heard about his sickness.

'I heard he had gone hunting not very long back. That is a good sign. I am sure he will make a quick recovery,' James repeated then, willing himself to believe it. 'He is much too strong to succumb to a mere fever.'

As it turned out, James was wrong. Strong and resilient though the Prime Minister had always been, this time it seemed as though his luck was running out. As the days passed, the fever raged on[138], finally rendering him completely incoherent one night. So much so, that he rambled on through the night, muttering and murmuring disjointed things that nobody could understand. He in turn, could recognize no one, refused to cooperate with the nurses or doctors, and by the time most of the night had passed, his temperature had gone up to an alarming level and Aristu had started hallucinating. The doctors had been closely monitoring his condition, but by then, even they had to give up. It was clear to everyone that he wouldn't make it and early that morning, he succumbed to the fever and passed away in his palace. Mu'inud-Daulah, Mushirul-Mulk, Azamul-Umara, Aristu Jah, the *Diwan* to Nizam Ali Khan (Asaf Jah II), died on 9 May, 1804,[139] leaving behind a legacy that could never be replaced. He had been Prime Minister of Hyderabad for twenty-six glorious years.

Aristu Jah was buried at the underground family tomb, about a kilometre and a half from the city. He had been a remarkably able politician and had wielded the kind of power few men can. Among his many accomplishments was his skilful negotiation of terms with the Marathas after the Battle of Kharda which had earned him the respect of the Nizam as well as of the people. It was no wonder that the title "Aristu Jah" had been bestowed on him, which means Aristotle of the time.[140] If anyone deserved the title, he certainly did.

---

138 Kugle, Scott. *When Sun Meets Moon – Gender, Eros and Ecstasy in Urdu Poetry (Islamic Civilization and Muslim Networks).* USA. University of North Carolina Press. 2016.

139 Hyderabad, Deccan, Central India, Late 17th Century. Art of the Islamic and Indian Worlds. Christie's. Live Auction, 2008.

140 Akbar, Syed. Over 20 historic maqbaras lose their land to grabbers. *The Times of India.* 23 July 2017.

'It was attended by throngs of people, family members, ministers, omrahs, citizens,' said James to Khair when he returned to the Residency after the funeral. 'They all sang his praises and talked about what a capable, powerful politician he was.' He paused; his voice almost breaking. 'For me though, he was always my dear friend "Solomon".'

Khair looked at James worriedly. After the Nizam's death, this loss was almost too much to endure. She tried to take him into her arms, but James was too upset to be comforted even by her this time. His eyes were glistening and he turned his face toward the bedroom window.

'He was too closely bound to the Nizam,' said Khair gently then. 'It is almost as though the Nizam's death signalled the beginning of the end for him too.'

'It is the end of an era.' James threw his head into his hands and shook it. 'It is almost impossible to believe that anyone would or could take his place.'

'Well, someone will.' Khair's voice was barely audible and her husband finally raised his eyes to meet hers. 'And I think we both know who it will be.'

'Impossible!' James seemed to momentarily recover from his melancholy mood as he stared at Khair in astonishment. 'After the way he has been disgraced! Besides, have you not heard about him lately? Well, I have. Apparently, he has been so badly affected by leprosy that people can hardly stand to look at him.'

'I have a feeling.' Khair smiled sadly. 'There is no point denying it.'

James stared at her for a few minutes and then stroked his chin thoughtfully. 'I suppose you are right. This is politics. And anything is possible in politics. Of course, as Resident, I will be asked to carry out a due diligence.'[141] Pausing, he nodded slowly. 'And I will have to be fair and unbiased. My government will expect that.'

'Speaking of politics, sometimes I wonder how...how...' Khair trailed off, not knowing how to put something so dreadful in words, but James nodded. Just like she could read his mind, he too could read hers.

'I wonder too. A healthy, robust man like Solomon. What was this mysterious fever that took his life so suddenly? I cannot help but marvel at something so uncanny.'[142]

'Well, we are not the only ones wondering. People have been talking. Everyone knows he made a lot of friends in his life, but he made some enemies too.' Khair placed her hand soothingly on her husband's. 'He is gone. Nothing can bring him back now. Try not to worry too much, Eshgham. You have not been well. Besides, we cannot stop the inevitable from happening, can we now?'

The power of female intuition was proved not long after, when Sikander Jah announced that Aristu Jah's former private secretary, Mir Alam, would indeed be taking his place as Diwan of Hyderabad.[143] This decision had been essentially influenced by the British, but despite the formal announcement, it was impossible to believe that a man so sick and who had been banished from the city in such disgrace, could be entrusted with such an enormous

---

141 Chancey, Marla Karen. *In the Company's Secret Service.* Thesis. Florida State University Library. 2003.

142 Kugle, Scott. *When Sun Meets Moon – Gender, Eros and Ecstasy in Urdu Poetry (Islamic Civilization and Muslim Networks).* USA. University of North Carolina Press. 2016.

143 Ali Khan, Raza. *Hyderabad 400 Years.* Hyderabad, India. Zenith Services. 1991.

responsibility. In fact, it wasn't only James and Khair who had been astonished at his appointment. Anyone who saw Mir Alam, marvelled at the decision. The leprosy that had afflicted him was one thing, but the rancour that was now so clearly etched across his face was evident of the fact that he still harboured an implacable grudge against everyone who had wronged him. As far as he was concerned, the tables had now been turned. And with Aristu Jah and the Nizam gone, Mir Alam clearly had his knife out for James. It was payback time.

With two of his dearest friends gone and the thrones of command in Hyderabad as well as Calcutta being occupied by people who clearly had a vendetta against him, James was disillusioned and disheartened with his prospects. He turned to other things, things which gave him solace. Khair and the children proved to be enormous pillars of support and with the renovation work at the Residency steadily moving forward, there was plenty for him to do. He spent more time gardening, playing with his children or watching the stars from the new observatory on the roof. Khair and he still socialized with friends and relatives, though it was more difficult now, with James's health deteriorating fast. Sometimes, he had to spend entire days in bed because of the painful rheumatism or the hepatitis. During that time, Aziz Ullah and Henry Russell remained his loyal friends, frequently reporting to him about news from both Calcutta as well as the Nizam's durbar. News about the possibility of Wellesley being in trouble was coming in more regularly now. James was aware of the fact that the Company's Board of Directors were not pleased with the Governor General's aggressive approach and were seriously thinking of recalling him. True, Wellesley represented the Company's shift from being a trading entity to an imperial power. After all, he had managed to annex huge Indian territories to the British and helped establish British domination around the country. So much so, that a few months later a young officer in the Company's judicial service even wrote, "An Englishman in India is proud and tenacious, he feels himself a conqueror amongst a vanquished people and looks down with some degree of superiority on all below him."

However, it was also a fact that the wars and conflicts had cost the Company dearly and embarrassed the home authorities. Before Wellesley was appointed as Governor General, the British had followed a policy of consolidating their gains and resources in India, but making territorial gain only if it did not antagonize the major Indian rulers. Wellesley, on the other hand, had openly pursued his political aspirations of subjugating Indian rulers by relying on three methods – Subsidiary alliances, the assumption of territories of previously subordinated rulers and outright war. This had worked as far as establishing the Company's position and authority in India was concerned, but it did not change the fact that Wellesley's policies had proved exceedingly costly and reduced the Company's profitability. The expenses of war had depleted the treasury and the Company's debt had increased exponentially over the last few years, from seventeen million pounds in 1797 to a staggering amount that had the shareholders extremely concerned. The fact that the Company's resources were getting drained at a time when Napoleon was again becoming powerful in Europe, wasn't ideal either. British statesmen and the Directors of the Company felt that taps had to be turned off as far as needless expenditure was concerned, further expansion had to be checked and that it was time to digest and consolidate the Company's recent gains. Of course, Henry Dundas having left the Board in 1801 further weakened the Governor General's position. Now, it really did seem as though he had finally lost the support of the Board and that the time had come for him to be recalled and someone more benign to be appointed in his place.[144]

James was therefore not surprised when the confirmed news about Wellesley being recalled and Lord Cornwallis replacing him reached him. Good news had indeed come after a very long time. James's prospects at last, did not seem quite as bleak as before and for the first time in months, he began to wonder whether it was the end or the beginning.

144 Campbell, Ryan. La Salle University. *The Histories. Richard Wellesley and the Fourth Anglo Mysore War.* Volume 15, Issue 1. 2019.

20
Flown Away

Ever since he'd first come to Hyderabad and assumed the position of Resident, James had always received ready cooperation from the Nizam's durbar. He was aware of the fact that it was this support that had allowed him to succeed in his key responsibility as a diplomat. Now, for the first time in years, James understood how simple jobs could become herculean tasks, only on account of the resistance that he was facing from the durbar. The durbar that had always seemed like a friendly place where he was welcomed with open arms, now reeked of hostility and antagonism. As Prime Minister, it was Mir Alam's responsibility to provide cooperation and support to the Resident, but he instead used his position to settle all his personal scores with James. For his part, James did try to make peace with Mir Alam, but the Prime Minister was too bitter from the past to be receptive. James finally gave up, once again diverting his attention to his family life and the changes taking place in Calcutta. They were well into the new year by then and with Wellesley on his way out and Cornwallis ready to take the place of Governor General, there would most certainly be several policy changes in the Company. James wasn't sure how this would affect him but he was admittedly, carefully optimistic. Everyone knew that Lord Cornwallis did not agree with most of Wellesley's principles.

Besides, James was convinced that nobody could loathe him as intensely as Wellesley had. Any change was likely going to be good for him.

Time seemed to be passing at a very swift pace, but unfortunately, James's health was also declining equally rapidly, and in February that year he decided to take action on something he'd been seriously considering for a while. A particularly bad episode triggered by the hepatitis which left him with a pain so acute that he was almost gasping for breath, was what ultimately drove him to it. At forty, he was still young but considering his circumstances, James didn't want to take the chance. He had to protect his innocent children, after all. And so, one day, he mustered up all the energy he could, gathered his thoughts and started writing out his will. Knowing that Khair possessed huge wealth in the form of land and jagir, in addition to her jewellery which in itself was a fortune, he left her only a token bequest, with his love and respect. He did express his complete devotion to her, and then went on to leave significant fortunes to his two children, Ali and Noor.[145] There was no mention of any other lady in the document, which was not surprising. James may have had many women in his life, but his complete devotion to Khair-un-Nissa had been distinctly clear from the day she had entered his life. He did also leave large amounts of money to his niece and nephew, and expressed his gratitude to his brother William, for everything that he had done for him over the years, including launching his career with the Company and the love and affection he had shown

145 Original Will of Lieutenant Colonel James Achilles Kirkpatrick. The National Archives. United Kingdom. (Scan QR code in References for the complete will.)

him. Needless to say, James felt immense relief, now that the will had been written and sealed.

There was of course one other major event which James and Khair had to start preparing for; a very heart-breaking one. Later that year, the children were to be sent off to England to study. James and Khair had been talking about it, but it was only in March that year, that the reality of the impending departure struck them. Suddenly, it felt as if they had no time left. Khair particularly, now seemed to be counting each day with a growing sense of trepidation.

'I see you have been looking distressed lately,' James remarked to her one evening as they strolled together in one of the flower gardens. James had had the gardeners plant an assortment of night blooming flowers, including the iridescent moonflowers that they both loved and their heady fragrance always reminded them both of that first evening in the garden behind his study. Today, however, all Khair could think about was the children's approaching departure.

'You know me very well Eshgham,' said Khair then. 'But how can I not be distressed? They are still so small, the thought of them going away terrifies me.'

'You know it has to be done.'

'Yes, of course it has to be done.' Khair's eyes were glistening with unshed tears. 'After all, only a proper upbringing on English soil can protect them from the prejudices that so many Anglo-Indian children are subjected to. No matter if I never get to see my children again.'

'Of course, you will be able to see them.' James tried to re-assure her.

'I may never see them again,' Khair repeated, shaking her head. It was what she feared the most.[146] 'And even if I do, they will be unrecognizable to their own mother!'

'It is the custom. And the younger they are, the easier it will be for them to adjust to new surroundings and a new way of life.'

Khair smiled bitterly. 'I know, it is the custom. Tell me Eshgham, why have we always been the victims of such customs? Customs that threaten to destroy everything we have built, everything that we live for. Why?'

James was silent and Khair shook her head. 'I know I ask you too many questions. Questions that you simply cannot answer. I know I push you too much, I always have.'

'It is what I love about you.' James took her hand and kissed it. 'Do not torment yourself anymore. Inshallah, I promise you, we will soon go to England together to see them.'

'England?' Khair laughed disbelievingly. 'I have never even been out of Hyderabad.'

'Well, there is always a first time for everything.' James slipped his arm around her shoulders and drew her close. 'What is so incredible about it? Plenty of Indian women accompany their husbands to England. I daresay, we will not be the first ones.'

'Thank you.' Khair smiled up at him lovingly. She didn't know if it would ever happen, but the promise itself was precious to her.

There was a short silence as they continued their stroll. James had been feeling a little better that day and was enjoying just being with Khair. Spring was now well on its way in, but the night temperatures, particularly in the gardens, were still cool.

---

146 Gilmour, David. *The British in India: Three Centuries of Ambition and Experience.* Penguin. August, 2019. United Kingdom.

'When will they be leaving?' Khair broke the silence. She knew it was now not a matter of "if" but "when". The separation was inevitable.

'I will book them passage on the Lord Hawkesbury.[147] It leaves Madras in September. Dr Ure and his wife will accompany them to Madras, so they will be taken care of. We will also arrange for an English nanny to travel with them to England. They can stay in Madras for a few weeks with my aunt and uncle.' He did not tell Khair that he was also intending to commission the English painter, George Chinnery, to do the children's portrait while they were in Madras.[148] He meant it to be a surprise for her. Ali and Noor had never had their portraits done and James was confident that Chinnery would do a marvellous job. Born in London, Chinnery had attended art school there and had then moved to Dublin as a portrait artist. He had, in fact, also painted a self-portrait which had been exhibited at the Royal Academy, London, in 1798.[149] After tasting some success in Ireland, Chinnery had now established himself in Madras. Believed to be somewhat hypochondriacal, Chinnery was certainly a temperamental and eccentric man, but then wasn't eccentricity a characteristic of all good artists?

It was a warm day in the month of July when the children finally left. Unfortunately, their last weeks in Hyderabad hadn't been quite as memorable as James and Khair had hoped they would be. James's

---

147 Meaden, David. *Hidden Letters: When Documents Contain a Surprise.* Untold Lives Blog, British Library, India Office Records.

148 Swami, V. Narayan. *A Many-tinted, Radiant Aurora: George Chinnery's Kitty Kirkpatrick.* Books Society of India. 24 July 2014.

149 Self Portrait. George Chinnery. The Collection. European Paintings. The MET, New York. 1825-28.

health had suddenly taken a particularly bad turn, completely confining him to bed. Instead of spending time with his children before their departure as he'd intended, he'd spent most of those last days too weak to even visit the bathroom unaccompanied. As for Khair, she had never felt as torn in her life as she did then. One part of her wanted to spend every possible moment with her children, while the other part refused to leave her husband's bedside. It had certainly been a very heart-breaking time for the family. Now, as the palanquins that they were to travel in came to a halt outside the Residency entrance, the children clung to their parents, refusing to go. Too young to fully understand the enormity of their departure, and too old to be completely oblivious to it, the confused expressions on their small faces tore at their parents' hearts as they held the tiny bodies and hugged them for the last time. Khair was inconsolable. James and Sharaf-un-Nissa tried their best to comfort her, but they knew how traumatic it must be for a mother to see her children go away like this. Feeling utterly helpless, they stood and watched as she held on desperately to Ali and Noor.

'Ya Allah, Ya Allah!' she wailed, kissing the dimpled hands over and over again. 'I cannot bear this, I cannot. I would rather die!' They were standing on the portico steps of the Residency, the only home the children had ever known. Dressed in their traditional Hyderabadi clothes, they looked like they were going to visit friends or relatives in one of the palaces around Hyderabad. Not more than seven thousand kilometres away to a country they had never seen and a culture they did not understand.

'Let go Khair, let go!' James, deathly pale and weak from his illness, had managed to get himself out of bed to bid farewell to his children. Now he tried to pull Khair away from them and into his arms, but she would have none of it. Hugging her children close to her, she wept and wept, until even the Residency staff was crying along with her. Some of them couldn't help being surprised at the candid expression of emotion since this was not usual in the aristocracy. Khair was an exception in many ways. When other mothers had left the child rearing completely to nurses and nannies, Khair had been an attentive and loving mother, always involved with her children. To those who had seen her with her children, it seemed almost impossible that she would survive this separation.

Unable to get through to his wife, James turned to his mother-in-law. She was perhaps the only person who would be able to give Khair any comfort today.

Sharaf-un-Nissa's eyes were drenched with tears as she pulled her daughter into her arms and stroked her hair. The truth was that she wanted to tell her to stop them, to fight this injustice, to forsake this ridiculous custom that wrenched a mother away from her children like this. After all, she was a mother too. Who could understand Khair's pain better than her? 'Let them go, Khair Joon,' she said instead, knowing that it was no use. 'It is for their good, to give them a better future.'

'But how will I live without them? I will most certainly die!' An unabated river of tears was flowing down Khair's face and her entire body was shaking with huge wracking sobs as her mother tried to calm her down.

After what seemed like hours, the children finally got into the waiting palanquins with Dr and Mrs Ure. From the Residency, they would follow the Musi on to Masulipatam, from where they would take the boat to Madras. There, they would break the journey for a few weeks before boarding the ship for England. It was an arduously long journey for such small children, particularly those who had never before been outside the safe confines of their home. As for Khair, there she sat on the marble steps of the portico, watching the palanquins being lifted off the ground. Then they started moving, slowly at first, then faster, further and further away. The distance between her and the children kept growing until the palanquins were just tiny specks. Like two little birds, they had flown away from the nest, away to an unknown land where she couldn't go. 'But they are still so small,' she suddenly shrieked as the palanquins finally vanished from her sight. 'My babies, oh, my babies!' Lifting her hands from her lap, she began to tear at her beautiful, long hair, wrenching out entire handfuls. Her mother and husband rushed to stop her, but Khair was almost hysterical by then. She was hurting terribly, in places that she hadn't even known existed inside her. Whatever her mother said, whatever consolation or reassurance James tried to offer her, deep in her heart, in her soul, Khair-un-Nissa knew that she would never see her children again. They were gone.[150]

150 Gilmour, David. *The British in India: Three Centuries of Ambition and Experience.* Penguin. August, 2019. United Kingdom.

21
The Call of Duty

James looked at his wife, concern etched across his pale face. Khair had been sitting with her embroidery for over an hour, but the pattern hadn't progressed at all. It was almost lunch time, but as usual, they were still in the bedroom. Too weak and tired, James spent most of his time in bed these days and Khair had flatly refused to leave his side. She spent hours every day, sitting next to him in the sheesham rocking chair, working at her embroidery or reading a book. Sometimes, like the embroidery, the book did not progress beyond a page or two as she sat, holding it, staring vacantly into space.

'Do not look so serious, my dear.' With a smile, he now leaned over and kissed her on the forehead. 'You are much too young and beautiful to torment yourself so much.'

'I am fine.' She tried to smile back, but compared to the happy, easy smiles he had become used to, this was a very watery affair. It had been several days since the children's departure, but James couldn't remember the last time he had seen her smile properly.

'Is there something on your mind, Eshgham?' She placed the embroidery neatly on the table and James couldn't help thinking that as usual, she had managed to accurately read his thoughts.

Nodding, he leaned back into his pillows. He knew there was no easy way to talk to her about this. She was not going to approve. In fact, she was going to do everything in her power to stop him.

'The new Governor General has summoned me to Calcutta. I have to report as soon as I can.' His voice was soft, but there was a determination in his tone that told her he'd already made up his mind.

'But that is impossible!' Instantly, her listless demeanour gave way to an urgent alertness. 'The doctor has told you to take complete rest. How can you even consider going to Calcutta?'

'There are bound to be some major policy changes. Apparently, the Company is trying to salvage the situation and....'

'I do not care about all that.' Khair grabbed James's hand and clutched it to her chest. There was a sudden desperation in her eyes, the kind that James had only seen twice before. The first time had been when she'd realized that there were people like Mir Alam and Baqar-Ali-Khan who would have gone to any lengths to separate the two of them, and the second time when the children had left Hyderabad.

'Khair, my darling. You have to understand...'

'I understand nothing! I do not want to listen to this, I cannot...'

'This may be my very last chance to try and save my career. In fact, I have been advised not to delay at all.'

'You cannot even get out of bed these days.' Khair shook her head despairingly. 'Eshgham please...'

'I am an officer, Khair. I cannot forsake my responsibility. I cannot ignore the call of duty. Please do not ask me to do something I cannot.'

There was a silence as they both looked at each other, Khair still holding on tightly to her husband's hand. Weak and frail, James had barely made it out of bed for days. His forehead had been burning with a high fever since the previous day and he'd almost fainted in the bathroom last night. How could a man in that condition make a 1500 kilometres journey all the way to Calcutta? Then again, how do you ask an honourable, principled man to abandon his responsibilities?

'Cornwallis is a prudent man. Very different from Wellesley. It is a good thing that they did not come face to face, those two. Particularly after the mess that Wellesley has left in his wake.' James smiled, making an attempt at levity. He could not bear to see his beloved Khair looking so worried.

This time she smiled back and James was reminded of the first time she had smiled at him from behind that curtain. Sometimes he couldn't believe it had all started only six years ago. Instead, it felt as though they had spent a lifetime together. Shifting in the bed to make place, James held his arms out to his wife.

Khair rose from the rocking chair and joined him on the bed. Moving closer, she rested her head on his chest and his arms closed around her. She'd been spending almost every waking moment with him, but today, he felt unbelievably frail to her.

'The Company has already lost a great deal.' James shook his head. 'Money, resources, lives. They now want to change their image from an aggressive, acquisitive entity to a benevolent one that can co-exist with local forces. To do that, I suppose they need people like me.'

'Please Eshgham! Do not go!' The desperation was back in her voice. Stifling a sob, she wrung her hands together and pleaded. 'If anything should happen to you, I will most certainly die! First the children, now you! I will die Eshgham, I will die!'

'Nothing will happen to me, you will see.' James held her gently as she started to cry softly into his shoulder. 'Do not cry, my darling. That is one thing you know I cannot bear.'

They sat there for a long time, James holding her, Khair breathing in the fragrance of the sandal attar he always applied in the morning. For a while, nothing was spoken. Then finally, Khair broke the silence.

'When will you go?' As it had been with the children, she knew that now, it was not a matter of "if" but "when".

James sighed. 'As soon as I can get my things together. If I leave immediately, I might be able to make it to Madras before the children leave for England.'

'That would be nice.' Khair looked at him sadly. 'At least they will see one of us again.'

'They will see both of us one day. Inshallah, we will all be together again.' He placed the index finger and thumb of his right hand under her chin. Lifting her head ever so slightly, he smiled down at the beautiful woman who had instantly taken his breath away, the first time he had seen her. She'd seemed so unreachable, almost like a dream then. How far they had come.

'You should ask the valet to start making arrangements for your trip.' Khair tried to put on a brave face. 'If you want to get there before the children leave.'

'Yes, I will.' Nodding, James looked thoughtful. 'But there is one very important thing that I need to take care of, before I leave

Hyderabad. I must try and make peace with Mir Alam. This enmity cannot go on forever.'

The scene was disturbingly familiar, too familiar. The same piteous plea not to go, the assurances that they would soon meet again, the tearful farewell and then the portico steps where she sat and watched him leave. This time though, there was a horse instead of the palanquins since James would be riding all the way to Masulipatam. From there, just like the children, he would take a boat to Madras. For a man so sick and frail, it was going to be a nightmarishly difficult journey. Now Khair sat and watched wordlessly as he galloped toward the Residency gates. She had never before felt as alone in her life as she did just then.

'I am here, Khair Joon. I will always be here.' Almost as though she had read her daughter's thoughts, Sharaf-un-Nissa sat down on the steps and wrapped her arms around Khair. James was almost at the gates by then, but the sight of him going away, leaving, disappearing from her vision, was too much for Khair to bear. Leaning back into her mother's embrace, she closed her eyes and allowed the tears to fall. They were gone. All of them.

It was the West-East road beginning at the fort of Golconda that ran all the way to the port of Masulipatam. Despite being a land-locked town, Hyderabad had flourished enormously over the years, and it was the port of Masulipatam that was greatly responsible for that. After all, Masulipatam linked Golconda and Hyderabad to the world outside. Long before the Persians and the Europeans arrived there, it was the rulers of the Hindu Satavahana Dynasty who had set sail from this port. It was called Masalia then, before the name was changed to Masulipatam. What made this port so remarkable among the Coromandel ports was the commerce links that had been built with the West, Gujarat, the Persian Gulf and the Red Sea. For years, bullock carts and horse carts had carried precious stones, jewellery, textiles, tobacco and other high valued goods on the road leading to Masulipatam, making it one of the most significant roads in the region. Not surprisingly, Europeans had long competed for control of this strategically vital port. The Portuguese, the Dutch, then the French, and finally, the British.[151]

When James left the Residency, he took the same road and then started following the River Musi, toward the coast. Once he had left Hyderabad behind, James noticed that dry land gradually disappeared and wetter, damper coastland appeared in its place. The views changed considerably as the buildings, bazaars and monuments gave way to lush stretches of grassy land and swaying rice fields. Having lived most of his life in India, James was aware of the enormous role that paddy cultivation played in socio-cultural life, especially in festivals. Harvest festivals were both, a religious as well as a seasonal observance, particularly in the rural parts. And now that Hyderabad was behind him, these parts of Telangana were essentially rural. Hefty water buffaloes and oxen used in the farming of the fields became common sights, as did little huts by the side of the road where villagers congregated for a game of cards or a beedi. *Sari*-clad women with bright red *bindis* on their foreheads smiled

151 Baru, Sanjaya. Globalization of Golconda. Rediff. November 12th, 2007. Excerpted from the Waheeduddin Khan Memorial Lecture 2007, delivered at the Centre for Economic and Social Studies, Hyderabad on 30 August 2007.

coyly at him as he rode past, and sun-burnt, barefooted children frolicked in the muddy rain pools that always appeared this time of year. James had travelled this road before, but this time, he was in too much of a hurry to stop and admire the verdant countryside or even breathe in the heady aroma of lotus and magnolia blooms wafting in through the open expanses. On he galloped, barely able to think about anything other than the fact that time was running out. He'd been given this last opportunity to say goodbye to his children before they departed for England and he'd be damned if he missed this chance.

He finally reached Madras on 12 September. It had taken him several days and every ounce of his energy to make the trip. Unfortunately, though, the Lord Hawkesbury had sailed three days back, taking the children with it. It was only when James reached Madras, in an exhausted and ill state, that he realized that he'd missed his children by a mere three days.[152] Three days! It did feel like a very cruel blow of fate to him, almost as though destiny had completely turned against him. Disheartened and dejected, James then went on to spend a very lonely two weeks in Madras. It was with a heavy heart and a feeling of deep disappointment, that James concluded his time in Madras and finally boarded the ship for Calcutta.

152 Laslocky, Megan. *The Little Book of Heartbreak: Love gone wrong through the ages.* USA. Plume, a member of Penguin Group, USA. January, 2013.

22
Broken Promises

When James's ship docked at Calcutta, he was extremely sick. Barely conscious, in fact. He was running a very high temperature and was unable to walk on his own. Those who carefully carried him out of the ship could hardly believe that he was even alive. Some people though, did think that they heard him muttering something, but they weren't sure. James had been rendered almost delirious with the fever by then and the words were completely indiscernible.

'I think he said something that sounded like "hair, hair" but I can't be certain,' whispered one Englishman to his wife. They'd been James's co passengers on the ship, but this was the first time they had seen him. Let alone socializing with the other passengers, James had been too ill throughout the trip to even step out of his cabin.

The lady leaned closer to her husband. 'No, it was not "hair, hair" but "Khair, Khair". She must be a lover or a wife,' she said softly.

They watched as James was carried out to shore. His complexion was bluish-grey and he was shivering uncontrollably, despite the hot and humid weather of Calcutta. 'He really is not going to make it, is he?' asked the wife then, glancing at her husband.

'I never saw that pallor on a man who made it.' The husband shook his head. 'It is strange that he was travelling in that condition.

I suppose it must have been a critical situation. Why else would such a sick man get on a ship? Poor ol' fella, it is a pity that he seems to have made the trip for nothing.'

What the man didn't know and neither did James, was that the trip had indeed been a completely wasted one, but for more reasons than one. James's condition was critical, but the man who had called him to Calcutta, the very reason that James had decided to risk his life and board the ship, was now dead. Charles Cornwallis, first Marquee and second Earl Cornwallis, had been sent to India to improve the administrative situation and establish peace, but he would never be able to accomplish his goal now. A significantly older man than he'd been the last time he'd come to India, the stressful work, travel and hard weather conditions seemed to have taken a toll on him. He'd been visiting the city of Ghazipur in the Northern state of Uttar Pradesh when he was suddenly struck by a fever. He couldn't recover and passed away at Ghazipur on 5 October 1805,[153] just days before James's ship docked at Calcutta. James, of course, hadn't known this and he continued to be completely unaware of the futility of his trip even as his condition worsened and he slipped into a coma. He never really awakened from his comatose state and lasted all of a few hours after that.[154] Those who saw him during those last hours could tell how much he was suffering, both because of the illness which ultimately took his life, as also from the lack of his loved ones around him. The palpable pain he was in was one thing, but it was also heart-rending to see how much he longed, yearned, to hold his begum and

---

153 Elevation of a proposed mausoleum for Lord Cornwallis in Ghazipur. Online Gallery. British Library.

154 Laslocky, Megan. *The Little Book of Heartbreak: Love gone wrong through the ages.* USA. Plume, a member of Penguin Group, USA. January, 2013.

his little children in his arms one last time. A man who had given and received so much love in his lifetime, was completely alone and surrounded by strangers as he finally breathed his last and left the world on 15 October.[155] It had been many years of suffering followed by a painful death. None of the people who had loved him were even aware of what had happened. His father, his brother, his two little children on board the Lord Hawkesbury, were all completely oblivious to the fact that James Achilles Kirkpatrick had slipped into a coma and died. And as for his begum, young, beautiful, frightened Khair, she had no way of knowing that everything she had feared, really had come true. She had no way of knowing that the love of her life, her husband, her Eshgham, was being lowered into the ground by strangers in a cemetery 1500 kilometres away, even as she sat and anxiously waited for news in the beautiful Rang Mahal that he had built for her. News that would tell her that he was safe. News that would now never come.

'Khair Joon, news has come for you.' Sharaf-un-Nissa entered Khair's bedroom, holding an envelope in her right hand. 'From Calcutta.'

With a smile, she held the letter out to Khair. She knew how anxiously Khair had been waiting and she hadn't wasted a single second to bring the letter to her.

'*Alhamdulillah! Alhamdulillah!*' Khair rushed over to her mother, almost tripping over the bed in her haste. The days since James had left, had passed in a hazy stupor. Not allowing her mind to think

155 Holmes and Co. The Bengal Obituary: Or a record to perpetuate the memory of departed worth, being a compilation of tablets and monumental inscriptions from various biographical sketches and memoirs of such as. India. Palala Press. 2016.

lest it wander into precarious places, she'd been going through the motions of her days on auto pilot. She ate her meals sometimes without even knowing what was on her plate, sat with her embroidery for hours without managing a single stitch, even the bangles that had always been her favourite pastime did not fascinate her anymore. Her mother and even the Residency staff had tried their best to offer support and keep her distracted, but all Khair wanted was news. And now it had finally come.

She grabbed the letter from her mother's hand. 'What took him so long? He should have known I would be worried sick. Oh, I hope he is well. I do hope the journey was not too much for him.' Even as she tore open the envelope and unfolded the letter, the first thing that came to her mind was that the letter hadn't been written by James. 'This is not his handwriting,' she murmured with a puzzled look. Shaking her head, she quickly scanned the first lines.

Deeply regret to inform you of the tragic passing away of Lieutenant Colonel James Achilles Kirkpatrick on Tuesday, 15 October, 1805 due to a high fever and delirium. His last rites were conducted on the same evening with full military honours. He slipped into a coma just hours before his death and...'

In an instant, the room spun around Khair and her legs gave way from under her. Sinking to the floor, she clutched her chest with her left hand, crumpling the letter in the other. Her face was contorted into a mask of horrified disbelief and her mouth was open, as though she was desperately trying to give birth to a scream, a scream that wouldn't come.

Watching her daughter collapse, Sharaf-un-Nissa rushed to her. 'Khair Joon!' She gathered Khair in her strong arms and shook her gently. Still holding the crumpled letter in her fist, Khair was vigorously shaking her head from side to side, as if trying hard to dispel a thought, an image from her mind. Still no sound came from her, but her eyes were wide open, the pupils dilated.

'Khair Joon! Khair Joon!' This time her mother shook her more firmly. Her own heart was beating painfully in her chest, but Khair looked as though she was in shock. 'Give me that letter!' She took her daughter's hand in her own. It was ice cold. Prising open the fingers, Sharaf-un-Nissa wrenched out the crumpled letter. Not waiting to smoothen it out, she unfolded it with one hand and started reading. Her other arm was still wrapped firmly around her daughter's shoulder, but she felt it waver for just a minute as the enormity of what was written in the letter finally hit her. Closing her eyes, she moaned softly. 'Ya Allah, Ya Allah!' Her voice was barely a whisper and she tightened her grasp on her daughter's body. 'Oh, my child, my dear child!'

Khair suddenly began to rock hysterically in her mother's arms. 'Why him, why? It's a lie, a cruel lie!' she shrieked, slamming the palm of her hand on her forehead. Tears had started flooding her eyes, but she didn't even bother to wipe them away as they fell and rolled down her cheeks in a continuous stream. 'Eshgham, Eshgham! I told you not to go, I told you!'

'Khair Joon, please....'

'He promised!' Turning to her mother, Khair grabbed both her hands. 'He promised me he would return soon! He promised that we would go and visit the children in England together! He promised to love me forever! So many broken promises, Maman Joon! So many broken promises!'

'No Khair Joon. He loved you more than anything. You have to know that.' By then, both women were holding each other and sobbing. Sharaf-un-Nissa looked at Khair, her heart weeping for the anguish she knew her child was going through. Khair looked as though her world had come to an end. And Sharaf-un-Nissa knew that it had. It really had. And what about the children? How small they were, how innocently oblivious to the tragedy that had befallen them. What would happen to them, now that their father was gone? As for Khair, she was so young; she should have her entire future in front of her. But the love that James and she had shared was different, extraordinary. It was the kind of love Sharaf-un-Nissa had never seen before. The kind of love that fills the being, the heart, the soul, so entirely, so completely, it leaves no room for anything else. And with James gone, Khair's heart was now empty, barren, filled with nothing but the enormous void that he had left behind.

Hours passed as Khair wept and wept against her mother's bosom. As she held her shattered, broken daughter in her arms and stroked her hair, urging her, begging her to calm down, Sharaf-un-Nissa couldn't help but wonder how Khair would ever endure this loss, the loss of her husband, her James, her Eshgham, the only man she had ever loved. And even though she knew that Khair's thoughts were only for James, Sharaf-un-Nissa's thoughts turned toward Khair, the one he had left behind. Undoubtedly, the road ahead was going to be an agonizingly arduous and lonely one for her. And the struggle, the strife, the torments that awaited her now that her husband, her protector was no longer there. Sharaf-un-Nissa didn't even want to think about it. The questions, the uncertainties were countless. Would she ever be able to see her children again? They'd heard stories of other Anglo-Indian children who'd been sent away and made to forever sever ties with their Indian families. How would the British now treat Khair? She was the legally wedded wife of the late Lieutenant Colonel James Achilles Kirkpatrick, but the conversion and marriage had been a very private affair. Would questions be raised about the legitimacy of the marriage? And with Mir Alam occupying the position of Prime Minister of Hyderabad, would the durbar offer any protection? James had tried to make peace with him before he left Hyderabad, but Mir Alam was like a snake, his promises meant nothing. Everyone knew that he did not forget or forgive easily, everyone had seen what he had done to Aristu Jah's family after his death.[156] The thought of it made Sharaf-un-Nissa shudder. Khair was just nineteen, after all! Would the world be fair to her or would they suddenly turn against an unfortunate, helpless young girl who had, in one brutal stroke of rotten luck, lost everything?

---

156 Dadabhoy, Bakhtiar K. *The Magnificent Diwan: The Life and Times of Sir Salar Jung 1.* India. Penguin Random House. 13 December 2019.

23
The City of Palaces

'Are you sure about this *Azizam*? What you are suggesting does not, by any means, sound easy.' Durdana Begum looked at her granddaughter sceptically and then glanced at Sharaf-un-Nissa. 'What do you feel?'

The younger woman smiled. 'You know me Maman Joon. I have always encouraged my daughters to follow their dreams, to go where their hearts lead them. How can I deprive her of this?'

'I just do not want you to feel pressured.' Durdana Begum leaned forward and spoke to Khair directly. 'I do not want you to think that you do not have a home anymore. Just because that Sydenham has taken over the Residency and asked you to vacate it, does not mean you are homeless Azizam. You will always have a home with us here.'

Khair looked around the room she had grown up in. It felt familiar and strange all at once. After all, her whole life had changed since the last time she had stayed here. Did it still feel like home? She wasn't sure. But then the Residency didn't feel like home either. The new Resident, Thomas Sydenham had ensured that. The home that James and she had lovingly built together, the warm abode that they had shared with each other and their children, now seemed like an unfamiliar, cold place where she did not belong. Everything had been changed, the furnishings, the customs, the staff. It was almost as though the new Resident was on a pressing mission to wipe out every trace of James's existence, his legacy. Even Aziz Ullah, James's loyal munshi, had been dismissed. That, in fact, had been one of the first things Sydenham had done after taking over as Resident. To add to that, was Sydenham's candid admiration and support for Mir Alam.[157] Things had certainly not been easy.

Khair sighed. She had never felt as rootless as she did now. Where should she go? She did not know. All she knew for certain was that for now, Calcutta was where she needed to be. She hadn't had a chance to even say goodbye to him. This would be like a final goodbye.

'Do not worry, Maman *Bozorg*.' Trying to smile, Khair squeezed Durdana Begum's hand gently. 'I shall not be alone. Maman Joon and Aziz Ullah will be with me. Not to mention, a sizeable entourage. Also, Henry Russell is in Calcutta and will be there to help us settle.'

'Why is he there?' Durdana Begum frowned. 'I thought he was supposed to be the Resident's Private Secretary.'

'I do not think Thomas Sydenham is going to make it easy for Russell to stay,' said Sharaf-un-Nissa. 'But that is hardly surprising, considering how loyal Russell was to Hushmat Jung. Do you know, he even managed to procure that portrait of the children for us? Chinnery completed it before the children left for England. Well, Russell sent it to Khair and we are taking it with us to Calcutta.'

Khair nodded. James had been correct in commissioning the portrait to George Chinnery. It was an oil on canvas and the use

157 Briggs, Henry George. *The Nizam: His History and Relations with the British Government*, Vol 2. India. Forgotten Books (A London based publisher of rare books). November, 2018.

of colour was brilliant. Ali and Noor were dressed in traditional Hyderabadi clothes with strings of pearls around their necks and red and gold *jootis* on their feet.[158] Noor had her arm around her brother's shoulders and Chinnery had captured the innocence of youth, that alluring childishness, that wistful look, so perfectly in the expressions of both the children. The beauty of the portrait was only one thing, though. The lost, forlorn expressions on her children's faces tore at Khair's heart and instantly brought tears to her eyes every time she saw the portrait.

'That was nice of him,' murmured Durdana Begum then. 'Still, I cannot help but worry. It is going to be a long journey for two women. When are you leaving?'

'As soon as possible.' Khair looked pensive. 'There does not seem to be anything left in Hyderabad for me, at least for now.'

'Hyderabad is your home, Azizam.' Durdana Begum shook her head. 'I know it has been terrible with everything that Mir Alam and Sydenham are doing, but it will always be your home. You cannot refute that.'

'Well, it may be home, but my destination for now is Calcutta.[159] And I must be on my way.'

It was way back in the early sixteenth century that the Portuguese first used the port of Calcutta to anchor their ships. Then, on 24 August 1690, Job Charnock, an employee and trader of the British East India Company, arrived on the muggy banks of the Hooghly

158 Garcha, Ciara. *The Curious Case of Kitty Kirkpatrick.* Our Shared Cultural Heritage. August 4th, 2020.

159 Laslocky, Megan. *The Little Book of Heartbreak: Love gone wrong through the ages.* USA. Plume, a member of Penguin Group, USA. January, 2013.

river. At that time, the Armenians, Dutch, French, Danes and Portuguese were already established there. There was dense jungle surrounding the location on three sides and therefore, it was considered secure from possible enemy infiltration. Not long after, the location became a thriving riverine port, booming with muslin, jute and indigo trade.[160] Over time, economic activity continued to rise, transforming the port into a gateway for trade and commerce. It wasn't surprising, therefore, when The Port of Calcutta finally grew into the second largest and busiest port of the British empire, next only to London.

When the boat carrying the two begums finally docked at the Port of Calcutta, it seemed to both of them as though they'd been traveling for a very long time. It had certainly not been an easy journey, particularly for two ladies who had never before travelled outside the safe confines of their city. The flurry of activity they saw around them, did however manage to sufficiently distract them from their exhaustion. After all, Calcutta was a fascinating new world and the first sights of the city were always very impressive.

In fact, it was not only the first sights of the city that were remarkable, it was the city itself. In the year 1772, Governor General Warren Hastings abolished dual government, made Calcutta the capital of British India and shifted the treasury from Murshidabad to Calcutta. In January 1780, *Hickey's Bengal Gazette* became India's first newspaper, and then with the formation of the Asiatic Society of Bengal by Sir William Jones in 1784, intellectual life in the city flourished enormously. The economic, social and cultural life was also booming and not surprisingly, Calcutta was soon regarded as the hub of British India – "the second city of the British empire",

160 Basu, Kallol. What's in a name? *The Statesman*. 22 June 2022.

after London.[161] And in 1806, Calcutta was truly at the zenith of its splendour and glory. The opulence, the sophistication, the grandeur, it was dazzling to the eyes of all those who witnessed it. It was the kind of elegance and urbanity that beckons you toward it, that is difficult if not impossible to resist. The tony neighbourhood of Chowringhee was the main European residential area with its regal Palladian houses, beautifully manicured gardens and recreational centres. When the new Fort William was constructed in 1758, wealthy Europeans in Calcutta gradually started settling in the neighbourhood. English architects began exploring the area for construction and opulent houses started springing up, which actually later went on to give Calcutta the title of "City of Palaces"[162] or "The St. Petersburg of the East".

Khair had no time to even notice any of the wonders that the city had to offer. The young widow was expectedly, entirely focused on spending every waking moment at her late husband's grave. The distance from their house to the cemetery was short and she would set off early every morning, ready to spend the entire day there. She had waited a long time to say this final goodbye to him and she would sit there for hours by herself, weeping silently. Sometimes it was difficult to believe that the tall, handsome, aristocratic man she had instantly fallen in love with, was really gone and the tombstone in front of her was all that was left to remember him by. Other times, the memories of the last seven years would come rushing by, would take over her senses in a way that the present didn't seem

161 Biswas, Ranjita. An Accidental City. *Deccan Herald.* August, 2016.

162 Correspondent. Is Chowringhee older than Kolkata. *Get Bengal.* 13 August 2021.

real at all. Those walks in the flower gardens, the fragrance of the moonflowers, the whispering to each other in bed after making love, plaiting Noor's hair together, teaching Ali to walk. The endless conversations, the laughing, the playful teasing. How she longed to see those twinkling blue eyes, to thread her fingers through that curly blonde hair. The price of loving, the pain of losing, was truly indescribable. That was something that Khair-un-Nissa had learnt at a very young age indeed.

It was a few weeks after they had arrived in Calcutta that Sharaf-un-Nissa decided to speak to Khair about something that had been on her mind. They had just finished dinner and were lingering over paan and hookah one evening when she broached the subject.

'We have been here for several weeks, Khair Joon.' Sharaf-un-Nissa gently placed her hand on her daughter's. 'We cannot go on like this forever. Even if you do not want to go out yet, we can at least start receiving some visitors. Hushmat Jung's niece Isabella would like to see you and the Palmers have sent several messages that they would like to visit as well. It will do you good to meet some friends.'

'Yes, that is exactly what Russell said to me yesterday.' Khair looked thoughtful. Meeting Henry Russell for the first time had been strange. Despite Russell's consistent presence at the Residency, Khair had always remained in the zenana and had never formally been introduced to him. He hadn't felt like a stranger to her, when he had finally visited her here. Aware of the camaraderie that had existed between her late husband and Russell, Khair had instantly warmed to him. Since then, Russell and she had spent many hours together and Khair had found him to be an attentive and solicitous gentleman.

'He is a nice man,' Sharaf-un-Nissa said then. 'Very considerate.'

'I will always be grateful to him for sending me that portrait.' Khair blinked back tears and tried to smile. 'It is my most prized possession.'

'That was indeed very kind of him,' Sharaf-un-Nissa agreed. 'So, should we invite the Palmers to visit us soon?' It had been a deliberate attempt on her part to change the subject. She knew that talking about Ali and Noor was always very difficult for Khair. 'Your seclusion has gone on for too long, my dear.'

'I do not know, Maman Joon.' Khair shook her head. 'I do not feel completely prepared to meet people just yet. Perhaps it is still too soon.'

'The Palmers are not just "people", Khair Joon. They are not even just friends. They are family. Faiz is like a sister to you. It will be good for you to meet her.'

Leaning back into the carved ivory settee, Khair sighed and then nodded. 'All right Maman Joon. I suppose you are correct. It will certainly be good to meet the General and Faiz. After all, they loved James very much as well. Let us invite them over soon.'

Over the next few weeks, Khair met the Palmers several times. Admittedly, meeting them was a bittersweet experience for her. It was certainly wonderful to spend time with people who had been so fond of James, who had seen and felt the love that Khair and he had shared. On the other hand, being with them was also a painful reminder of the happy times the four of them had spent four years ago, when the General and Faiz had visited Hyderabad. Just seeing the General who James had regarded as a dear friend, a brother, brought instant tears to Khair's eyes, but she treasured the time she spent with them, knowing that they were among the very few people who understood the extent of her heartbreak and in their own way, shared her loss and grief.

She met James's seventeen-year-old niece, Barbara Isabella Buller, several times as well. Born in Fort William in Bengal, Isabella was the second daughter of James's brother William and his wife Mary Seton. She had recently married Charles Buller of Cornwall and lived in Calcutta with her husband.[163] Isabella was an extraordinarily beautiful young woman with a natural compassion about her. Khair and she weren't strangers to each other, in fact, they had written to each other many times. Moreover, since the age difference between them was only two years, they had much to talk about and easily took to each other. The fact that James had also been very fond of Isabella, made meeting her an almost therapeutic experience for Khair. Seeing her, reuniting with the Palmers, spending time with Henry Russell, it was like healing for her now. They were all people who James had been extremely close to during his lifetime.

Sharaf-un-Nissa was relieved to see Khair engaged with friends and family once again. She liked Isabella Buller very much and thought her a very charming lady. The Palmers, she regarded as family. However, she also couldn't help noticing the attention that Henry Russell lavished on Khair during those weeks. He seemed to be rather enamoured and had taken it upon himself to never leave the young widow's side. Sharaf-un-Nissa knew that with Khair's extraordinary beauty and effortless grace, this was hardly surprising

---

163 Barbara Isabella (Kirkpatrick) Buller, 1788-1849. Wikitree. Genealogy Website.

and any young man would be easily attracted to her. She was also well aware of the fact that Khair was heartbroken and lonely after James's death and needed a shoulder to cry on. She just wasn't sure whether it was wise for Henry Russell to offer his shoulder. After all, Khair was a widow and with the way the situation currently was in Hyderabad, it would be prudent to be as discreet and careful as possible. Mir Alam, despite the solemn promise he had made to James, was a foe and not one to be taken lightly. Nothing would make him happier than to see Khair suffer. What the British government would do in a difficult situation also remained to be seen. James had been a senior officer and diplomat, yes, but he had also made many enemies among his own people, enemies who had resented him for years and would now rejoice in the downfall of his widow.

'Ya Allah!' Exclaiming to herself, Sharaf-un-Nissa closed her eyes. 'This child of mine has already suffered so much! She has lost so much! How many more turbulent paths must she walk? How many more burdens must she carry? How much more must she endure, how much?'

Even as she cupped her hands, raising them upwards to evoke the mercy of god, Sharaf-un-Nissa knew that the answers would come to them in time. She did also know one other thing with the utmost certainty. Whatever hurdles Khair might have to cross, whoever may turn against her, however much life might test her, she would always have her mother with her, by her side, supporting her, holding her up.

24
In Exile

Rumours were beginning to trickle in. Mir Alam was not going to lay out the welcome mat. In fact, some were even saying that he was furious with the dishonour Khair-un-Nissa had brought on her family and community, and forgiving her was not something that he was even willing to consider.[164] Khair, though distressed at the news, was not surprised. After all, hadn't James and she spoken about this on the very day Mir Alam had been sworn in as Prime Minister? It was what they had feared, though they had also expected it. It would be a lie to say that they had not. Some may have thought that James's final peace offering had softened, even melted the Prime Minister's heart, but not she. Oh no, she knew how cold-hearted and merciless that man could be. The fact that he had used this opportunity and banished her from her home, from the city she had been born in, from the only world she had ever known, should not have astonished anyone at all. Circumstances had made the already cunning and bitter man even more resentful, and forgiveness and magnanimity were not on his agenda. Anyhow, the message was clear. Mir Alam was now hell bent on revenge, and Khair was not safe in Hyderabad while he was in power.

---

164 Laslocky, Megan. *The Little Book of Heartbreak: Love gone wrong through the ages.* USA. Plume, a member of Penguin Group, USA. January, 2013.

In fact, the general feeling was that the situation in Hyderabad was most certainly perilous, as far as Khair-un-Nissa was concerned. Even Russell's influence, and god knew he had tried to use it, didn't seem to be helping. Russell had reached out to Sydenham to use his authority to guarantee Khair's safety, but Sydenham had seen no reason to go out of his way, for who was Khair-un-Nissa to him that he should stick his neck out for her benefit? On the contrary, if the way he was making changes in the Residency was anything to go by, then Sydenham was most certainly not someone to be counted on. Of course, on Lord Cornwallis's death, a Provisional Governor General had been appointed in Calcutta, but from the very beginning, Sir George Barlow had aimed to step into the shoes of his deceased predecessor and had prioritized peace and harmony with the local forces. His policy as he described it was, "directed to the divesting ourselves of all right to the exercise of interference in the affairs of the native princes where we possessed it almost to an unlimited extent by treaty, and to the withdrawing from all concern whatever in the affairs of every state beyond the Jumna."

It was therefore clear that the British authorities in India were not interested in anything that would lead to antagonism, and were actually much more concerned about the detrimental impact that Khair's reputation and actions would have on Indo-British relations in the Deccan. She had caused enough trouble already! There was nothing more they could do for her. And so, with no one to offer protection or guarantee her safe return to Hyderabad, Khair found herself in one of the most uncertain situations of her life. She could not stay in Calcutta forever, for Calcutta was not home. On the other hand, with no British protection and the merciless Mir Alam in power, returning to Hyderabad was perilous. Where was she to go? What was she to do? For the first time in her life, the beautiful young noblewoman felt utterly helpless, dejected and completely at the mercy of others.

Finally, after having spent several months in the "city of palaces", Khair, her mother and the devoted Henry Russell, departed from Calcutta. With a sizeable entourage in tow, they set off toward Hyderabad, though they knew that for now, Hyderabad was out of bounds. And so, instead of returning to her grandfather's home where she belonged, Khair had to stop three hundred kilometres short of Hyderabad and find a home in a place she had never imagined she would have to stay in. After all, Masulipatam was a port of importance, yes, but like any port town, it had a humid, muggy climate which could be quite cheerless and even depressing at times. Furthermore, Masulipatam had a sizeable population of fishermen as is the case with many coastal towns. The damp weather conditions also served as a perfect breeding ground for a variety of tropical diseases and all in all, it was simply not an appropriate place for two begums from Hyderabad's ruling family to stay in. However, since they did not seem to have much choice in the matter, they had to make their peace with it and accept Masulipatam as home, at least for the time being.

A pall of gloom seemed to settle around them the day they moved into their new house. The two-storey mansion[165] might have seemed sufficient to many, even luxurious to some, but it was a far cry from the comfort and opulence that Khair and Sharaf-un-Nissa had been used to, first in their family deorhi, then in the Residency. Besides, living out of tents was one thing, but the permanence of a home in

165 Naidu, T. Appala. Masula Heritage Sites. *The Hindu*. 3 June 2007.

a town like this was quite another. It was understandably difficult for the two begums to believe that this really was their home now. Expectantly, Khair's feeling of depression worsened as the weeks passed and she realized that it was going to be a very lonely, very solitary existence for them in this town. Sometimes it almost felt to them as though there was not a soul, not a single person in the whole of Masulipatam they could even have a conversation with. For two ladies who had previously been surrounded by friends and relatives, and had always enjoyed a thriving social life, that kind of seclusion would naturally have seemed unbearable. For Khair particularly, the memories of the years she had shared with James and the constant thoughts about the children who had been wrenched away from her, did not allow her any reprieve. This took a toll on her health and state of mind, and her worried mother said as much to her one day. They had been in Masulipatam for several months by then.

'You need to look after yourself, Khair Joon. The dark shadows under your eyes are even deeper today.' It was evident that she wasn't taking care of herself, she looked worn out and pale all the time. Doctors hadn't been able to diagnose what, if anything, was physically wrong with her,[166] yet it was clear that all wasn't right either. Sharaf-un-Nissa though, was sure that Khair was heartsick. Heartsick over the losses of a lifetime, losses that she might never completely recover from.

'I understand that things have been very hard Khair Joon. Particularly since there has been no news at all about Ali and Noor.' Sharaf-un-Nissa knew that not a day went by when Khair did not yearn to hold her babies in her arms.

---

166 Stewart, Stanley. India's Sleeping Beauty Awakes. *The Times*, UK. 28 November 2010.

'Ali and Noor?' Khair laughed bitterly. 'They have probably already been christened with their new names by now. They must have new identities, new relations, new lives. I am sure their English family would like to wipe off every trace of their former lives so that they do not remember any of it, not even their own mother. With James gone, I do not have any hope of ever seeing them again. It might be better for them to forget me and carry on with their lives.'

'Children can never forget their mother.' Sharaf-un-Nissa stroked Khair's hair with her gentle hands. 'You must never lose hope, my child.'

'False hope can be a very cruel thing, Maman Joon.'

A despairing look was etched across the young woman's face. That was when Sharaf-un-Nissa noticed that there was something different about her eyes. Once sparkling and iridescent, they seemed to have a hopelessness, a bleakness about them now. As though all the life had been sucked out of them. At that moment, there was nothing Sharaf-un-Nissa wanted more than to be able to give some solace, some comfort to this daughter of hers who was obviously hurting so badly. But this was one time when she could do nothing for her own child. Never before had she felt as utterly helpless as she did then.

'And now the portrait is gone too!' Khair stifled a sob. 'I have lost my most prized possession, Maman Joon!'

'You never should have given it to Chinnery.' This time Sharaf-un-Nissa couldn't keep the anger out of her voice. Chinnery had borrowed the portrait from Khair to exhibit it, but he had not returned it to her.[167] 'It belonged to Hushmat Jung and after him, to you.'

---

167 Swami, V. Narayan. *A Many-tinted, Radiant Aurora: George Chinnery's Kitty Kirkpatrick*. Books Society of India. 24 July 2014.

'Russell is trying to get it back for me. Though I do not know if he will be able to.' Khair accepted the tumbler of water that her mother handed to her and sipped.

'Speaking of Russell, he has not visited recently. Is everything all right with him?'

It was true that Russell's visits had become more and more infrequent of late. Khair had also not been entirely oblivious to his tearing hurry to return to Hyderabad all those months back, particularly after the way he had remained by her side during and after Calcutta. Admittedly though, she still waited eagerly for news from him. Perhaps her loneliness and solitude had brought forth a desperation that she hadn't ever experienced before.

'I suppose he is much too busy with other things these days. I hear he is in Madras and you can imagine how engaging the social life there is. After all, it is one of the Presidency towns.' Khair shrugged, trying to appear nonchalant. Her mother though, knew her too well to be fooled by acts of bravado. Russell's abandonment was another blow to her already shattered daughter. Rising from her chair, she came around to wrap her arms around Khair.

'Inshallah, everything will be all right, my child. Do not worry. However furious, vengeful or bitter Mir Alam might be, enough time has passed. I am sure that soon one day, his heart will melt and we will return to our home. I am certain he will have mercy on an innocent girl who has lost everything. He will not banish us from our home forever, he will not!'

'He already did.' Khair shook her head despairingly. 'It is no use Maman Joon. You know he does not forget or forgive easily. And he has his knife out for me now. Nothing anyone says or does will change his mind.'

'Enough time has passed,' Sharaf-un-Nissa repeated then, even more firmly. 'Have faith, my child. Have faith.'

Unfortunately, that was not how Mir Alam saw it at all. The feeling of bitterness toward Khair-un-Nissa was still running too deep. He had suffered too much, directly or indirectly, because of her and he was not going to forgive her until the very end. He did not care that a young woman from his own family, a kind and gentle noblewoman who had done no wrong but suffered enough anguish to last many lifetimes, had been banished from her city and her home. The only thing he cared about was to make someone, anyone, pay for all the humiliation and shame he had to endure. If Khair-un-Nissa was the ill-fated one, so be it. As for Khair, with an uncertain, lonely future looming ahead, time truly seemed to have stopped for her. She might have started with counting the days, but as they turned into weeks and the weeks into months, the enormity of her losses seemed to hit her like never before. There were days when she longed to hear James's voice, and nights when she yearned to hold Ali and Noor in her arms. But they weren't there and every night, Khair went to bed alone. Then, she would close her eyes and dream of happier times with them. James and the children. The children! How would they look now? The last time she'd seen them, they'd been dressed in their traditional Hyderabadi clothes with their little *topis* and strings of pearls around their necks, but they probably only wore English clothes now. They would have forgotten all their Persian and would only be speaking English. Images of the years they'd all spent together as a family would then come and go fleetingly, like little will-o'-the-wisps that try as she might, she couldn't hold on to.

Sometimes, she dreamt of Russell too. Russell who had been so compassionate and attentive after James had died, but now she hardly ever even heard from him anymore.[168] His visits had stopped completely and even the letters had become painfully infrequent. She knew he must be having a good time in Madras, and she'd even heard some rumours about a certain Jane Casamaijor, the daughter of a Madras civil servant, but Khair didn't know what to believe anymore. And even though she hadn't spoken about it to anyone, Khair was not oblivious to the fact that it was Russell who was, at least partly, to blame for the shame and infamy that she was currently being subjected to. Yes, people in Hyderabad had been upset with her for years over her association with James. But then, over time, slowly, gradually, some sort of reluctant acceptance had been granted to them. Surely there had been some who had even felt pity for her after James's death. Perhaps, if she had made amends and chosen to live quietly, unobtrusively, like a widow ought to have, they might even have completely forgiven her. But rumours of her association with Russell had most certainly closed that door for her. If the criticism had been unrelenting then, it was ruthless now. If the gossip had been spiteful then, it was that much more vicious now. And of course, this time there was no James to shield her, no one at all who could protect her from those who wished to hurt her, destroy her. This time, there was no one.

---

168 Laslocky, Megan. *The Little Book of Heartbreak: Love gone wrong through the ages.* USA. Plume, a member of Penguin Group, USA. January, 2013.

25
Homecoming

It all looked the same. The marble arches, domes and porticoes, the plush Persian rugs on the floors of the main hall, the carved furniture in white and gold, the gleaming chandeliers adorning the ceilings. It was as though they had never left. At first of course, it had almost felt like a dream, a reverie, as she had just stood there, hesitant, uncertain, even a little disbelieving.

'She has not changed,' an aunt had remarked as they'd stood and watched her from a distance. 'See how she stands? The same delicate movements, the elegant stance. Like a small bird about to take flight.'

'Yes.' Sharaf-un-Nissa had shaken her head sadly. 'Only the wings were clipped long ago.'

Khair had started ascending the marble staircase then, the winding one that led up to the first and second floors. Slowly first, and then more certainly, as the images that had haunted her dreams gradually appeared and came into focus. The paintings on the walls, the carved windows that looked over the courtyards and gardens, the fruit trees below. Finally, she'd come to the corridor, the one that had always connected their rooms. Involuntarily, a small smile started playing on her lips as she remembered the tinkling sound her silver anklets had made when she ran across to her mother's room on the morning after her sister's wedding, to announce that she was madly in love with the Englishman. The one with the gentlest of smiles and eyes as blue as the sky. Had it really been more than a decade? Sometimes it seemed as though it had all happened only yesterday, the memory was still so vivid in her mind. Other times, it felt as though a lifetime had passed them by.

Just like the rest, the bedroom too had remained unchanged. She'd touched the bookcases still lined with her favourite books, run her fingers over the smooth sheesham table on which her mother had placed a glass of saffron milk every night for her to drink when she was pregnant, the chair by the window where she'd often sat and watched the Charminar, the heart of the city that she loved so much. Even as she looked around her old bedroom, Khair couldn't help remembering the day James had invited her and Ali to move into the Residency with him. That was the last time she had stayed here. But now, this was home again.

Undeniably, it was the news of Mir Alam's death that had cleared the way for Khair and her mother to finally return to their home.[169] Mir Alam of the Salar Jung family had served as Prime Minister of Hyderabad for only four years, but they had been the worst four years of Khair's life. In those four years, she had lost her children, her husband and her home. As for Mir Alam, it was the leprosy that had tortured him for years that had finally taken his life. Soon after his death, he had been buried at Daira Mir Momin Cemetery in the old part of the city[170] and a fresh water tank for which he had laid the foundation in 1804, had been named after him. The tank,

169 Laslocky, Megan. *The Little Book of Heartbreak: Love gone wrong through the ages.* USA. Plume, a member of Penguin Group, USA. January, 2013.

170 Asif Yar Khan. Here sleeps the earliest urban planner. *The Hindu.* 18 June 2013.

an engineering marvel with twenty-one semi-circular arches spread across an area of one mile, had been built by a French engineering company[171] and would undoubtedly be something that the late Prime Minister would be remembered by. Understandably though, it wouldn't be surprising if Khair-un-Nissa did not wish or intend to remember Mir Alam, if she could help it.

'Well, he has had his share of troubles too, Maman Joon. Particularly after his wife, Jane, passed away.'

'Indeed, a terrible tragedy! I heard she contracted a painful tropical disease.[172] She was so young, and he was quite distraught when she died. Apparently, he got rid of many things that reminded him of her. Furniture and such.' Sharaf-un-Nissa lifted the hookah pipe to her lips.

Khair sighed. 'Losing a loved one is always a tragedy, Maman Joon.'

Just then, a maid entered the room, bearing a tray. Even as she set it down at the table, a spicy aroma of cloves and cinnamon wafted up from the Shikampuri kebabs set out on a platter. They looked as delicious as they smelt, but Khair, who had no appetite for most things now, shook her head when her mother proffered the platter to her. 'I am not hungry.'

Sharaf-un-Nissa looked at her daughter gravely. She had thought that after returning to Hyderabad, Khair would begin to recover her health, but they had been here for many months already and she still

171 Correspondent. Mir Alam Tank Boating. Telangana Tourism, Dept of Telangana.

172 *The Russells of Swallowfield Park.* Swallowfield Park Case Study, UK. East India Company at Home, 1757-1857.

didn't look well. She had lost weight recently and the pallor of her face was far too pale. Even now the doctors were flummoxed. They couldn't diagnose anything that was specifically wrong with Khair-un-Nissa's health.[173] Yet it was palpable that all was not well either. She just didn't look like the girl her family had known before. There was something missing, something that seemed to have died, deep within her.

'You have to start eating better, my child. You need to take care of yourself.' After that, the older lady hesitated. But there was nothing wrong with what she wanted to say. After all, even the Koran had not forbidden the remarriage of widows. In fact, it had encouraged it as long as the four lunar months and ten days of Iddah were observed. And Khair! It pained Sharaf-un-Nissa to see her young, beautiful daughter living such a lonely life, devoid of love or companionship. But every time she'd spoken to her about remarrying, Khair had refused to even discuss it. Perhaps, the losses, the memories, were still too new. Maybe she needed more time.

'Anyway, coming back to Russell, I hear Charles is his Assistant now.'[174]

Khair's voice snapped her out of her thoughts and Sharaf-un-Nissa nodded. 'Yes. The two brothers make a good team. Charles is very loyal to Henry.'

Khair shrugged. She had known Henry closely during those months they had spent together in Calcutta and even though she might not have realized it then, she now understood that there was

---

173 Stewart, Stanley. India's Sleeping Beauty Awakes. *The Times*, UK. 28 November, 2010.

174 *The Russells of Swallowfield Park*. Swallowfield Park Case Study, UK. East India Company at Home, 1757-1857.

a domineering, patronizing side to his personality as well. It was also obvious that Charles as the younger brother, had for years, borne the brunt of Henry's domination.

'I hear he was willing to pay Sydenham a thousand pounds for his library,'[175] remarked Khair then. 'Though everyone says he has brought back many of James's ways at the Residency.'

'Yes, he has,' confirmed Sharaf-un-Nissa. 'Including strict adherence to the caste system in the kitchen.[176] But that is hardly surprising. Henry was very influenced by James. Almost like his protégé, in a way.'

Khair smiled wistfully. 'Well, it was always his dream to become Resident of Hyderabad. I am happy that he has finally realized it.'

Yes, Russell had finally realized his dream. He had always wished to be Resident of Hyderabad and now he was. The state of affairs in Hyderabad were going through a paradigm change over that period. After Mir Alam's death, he had been succeeded as Diwan by his son-in-law, Munir-ul-Mulk who turned out to be an ineffective prime minister. In fact, it was his *Peshkar*, a man of Hindu descent called Chandu Lal who was the real administrator. Very popular with the British, Chandu Lal had a submissive and deferential look about him, though he was also astute and intelligent. Unfortunately, instead of using his intelligence for the welfare of the state, he turned to corruption and managed to hold on to his position by being subservient to the British. Understandably, this was not a good

175 Finn, Margot. *Learning to Furnish.* Swallowfield Park. Warwick. East India Company at Home. 1757-1857.

176 Finn, Margot and Smith, Kate. *The Russells in India: Anglo Indian Tastes. East India Company at Home, 1757-1857.* UCL Press.

situation for the Nizam, Sikander Jah. He was not administratively strong like his father to start with, nor did he have a friend sitting in the Residency as James had been to Nizam Ali Khan. On the contrary, Henry Russell had no sympathy at all for the new Nizam. And so, with Russell on one side and Chandu Lal on the other, Sikander Jah did not have an easy time as far as governance was concerned.[177] And when his last attempt to remove Chandu Lal was refused by Russell, he took it as a personal blow to his ego and shut himself up in his palace. With the help of Chandu Lal, this allowed Russell to strengthen the Company's position in Hyderabad by firmly establishing what was later known as the Hyderabad Contingent. It was started as a force with two thousand soldiers and new posts were continually added over time, but the Nizam never used this force, despite paying heavily for it and eventually ending up in an enormous amount of debt. In any case, it was evident that the easy camaraderie and genuine warmth that had been witnessed between the late Nizam Ali Khan and James Achilles Kirkpatrick was a thing of the past. In fact, the Hyderabad that had existed then was now, a thing of the past. For Khair and Sharaf-un-Nissa though, nothing mattered anymore. They were just glad to be back home.

As it turned out, Khair did not marry again. Perhaps being abandoned by Henry Russell had disheartened and disillusioned her too much. Or perhaps the love she had shared with James, had been the kind that had filled her heart so totally, so completely, that there simply hadn't been any room left for anyone else's again. Maybe

---

177 Ali Khan, Raza. *Hyderabad 400 Years.* Hyderabad, India. Zenith Services. 1991.

it was the kind of love that a human being can only experience once in a lifetime and never again. And so, she continued to live quietly in the deorhi with her mother and the other women of the family. Sometimes when people met her, they saw a quiet, gentle, somewhat reclusive young woman who didn't smile much. But those who knew her, saw much beyond that. They saw her eyes, the eyes that now bore a thousand memories of a past lifetime, memories that would not allow her to forget, to move on. They saw her pain, the pain of the brave, beautiful girl who had once dared to defy everything and everyone for love. They saw the heart, the one that had been shattered when she lost that love, shattered into so many smithereens that there was no way to put it together again. And it seemed to them as though with every new dawn, the sun was setting a little more on Khair-un-Nissa. And as the days passed and she continued to waste away, it became clear to everyone that Khair-un-Nissa, "the best of women", would not survive much longer. Even her mother could deny it no more. Khair was dying.

Sometime in September 1813, after an estrangement and silence of over five years, Khair-un-Nissa finally wrote to Henry Russell. It was a simple, honest letter to let him know that she was dying. Of course, it was tragic to think that a beautiful, young, twenty-seven-year-old noblewoman would have to write a letter like that and perhaps Henry Russell too, was uncharacteristically moved by it. Or perhaps he was carrying with him some iota of guilt at what had happened between them all those years ago. Whatever the case, he answered her letter right away, inviting her back to the Residency, to spend her last days in the one place she had loved the most in the world.[178] Her beautiful Rang Mahal that her beloved James had made for her and where she had undoubtedly spent her happiest days with her husband and children.

Just like James had been carried out of the ship when it had docked at Calcutta, Khair too was much too weak and ill to walk herself and had to be carried into the Residency. Unlike James though, Khair was not among strangers in those last moments of her life. Her dearest friend, Faiz Baksh also happened to be in Hyderabad at the time and with Sharaf-un-Nissa on one side and Faiz on the other, Khair was surrounded with all the love in the world. With tender hands, she was carried into her beloved Rang Mahal and then further on, into her old bedroom. Even as she looked around with fading eyes, it was as though nothing had changed in there. At that instant, despite her dwindling faculties, it seemed to her as if she could hear James's voice, as clear and gentle as it had always been, speaking to her. '*Masha Allah*, you look so beautiful today, my darling Khair. That colour is truly resplendent on you.'

Khair smiled. It all felt so real. Even the sounds of the children shrieking and laughing, the voices of their nannies as they followed them down the long corridors, the steady ticking of the clock that used to hang in their bedroom, the heady fragrance of the moonflowers. It was all still there. Then, she was gently lowered into the same four-poster bed where James and she had often lain, talking, laughing, dreaming the hours away. The same bed where she'd given birth to her daughter, beautiful little Noor-un-Nissa, Sahib Begum. Khair remembered the first time she had held her in her arms and how James had whispered the Adhan in her right ear

---

178 Laslocky, Megan. *The Little Book of Heartbreak: Love gone wrong through the ages.* USA. Plume, a member of Penguin Group, USA. January, 2013.

and the Iqamah in her left. How tiny she had seemed. How happy they had been. With a sigh, she reached for her mother's hand.

In an instant, Sharaf-un-Nissa was bending over her daughter. 'Do you need something Khair Joon? Water? Anything?'

Khair shook her head. Hours went by as her mother continued to stand there, speaking to her, stroking her hair. The light was beginning to wane by then and things were becoming hazy, but Khair could see the tears glistening in Faiz's eyes, could feel the tremor of her mother's hand as it held hers. There were other people there too, talking, whispering, in hushed voices. Maybe they were doctors and relatives and the Residency staff, but she couldn't be sure. She didn't even know how much time had passed since she'd been lying there in her old bed, it was now difficult to be aware of much. The only thing she was conscious of, were the two women standing steadfastly on either side of her, two women who loved her and couldn't bear to let her go. One who had given birth to her and stayed constantly, unwaveringly, by her side all her life. And the other who had in the short time that she'd known her, become a soul sister, and maybe even far more than that. They'd both witnessed the love that James and she had shared, then had grieved along with her when she'd lost him and the children. Her mother and her best friend. Her two beautiful pillars. She had indeed been blessed to have them in her life.

Khair closed her eyes. Even as she started murmuring the first words of the *Kalima,* she could see visions of the years gone by. How many beautiful moments they had all spent together! Those evenings in her mother's room as they chatted over sherbet, cards or hookah, those long walks in the flower gardens with her beloved James, the glitter of the bangles that she'd presented to Faiz when she and the General had visited Hyderabad, the afternoons in the gardens outside Rang Mahal as they discussed their future and watched the children play. The children! Her babies! How she wished she could have seen them one last time, held them in her arms and told them how much she would always love them. But they were in a faraway land, in a world that was unknown to her. And now, she too was going to go away, to another strange world. Perhaps she would float up, higher and higher, up into the sky, the sky that was as blue as the eyes of the Englishman she had fallen so deeply in love with.

And she was gone. Hyderabadi noblewoman, Khair-un-Nissa, "the best of women", left the world on 22 September 1813. She was only twenty-seven years old then. By many, she would be remembered as the granddaughter of Baqar-Ali-Khan and Durdana Begum, the daughter of Mehdi-Yar-Khan and Sharaf-un-Nissa,[179] the wife of Lieutenant Colonel James Achilles Kirkpatrick and the mother of Mir Ghulam Ali, Sahib Allum and Noor-un-Nissa, Sahib Begum. But to the two women standing on either side of her, still holding the hands that were already too cold, she would always be their Khair, gentle and beautiful Khair, the brave young woman who had dared to defy and strived to live, for love.

179 Sharaf-un-Nissa. Geni. Genealogy.

Epilogue

Khair-un-Nissa was buried alongside her father's grave, in the city that had always been her home. Of course, it was tragic that her beloved husband was buried almost a thousand miles away from her. A couple who had challenged and defied everything and everyone to be together, had been separated in their final resting places.

The children, Mir Ghulam Ali, Sahib Allum and Noor-un-Nissa, Sahib Begum were brought up by their paternal grandfather in Hollydale, the Kirkpatrick family's ancestral home in South East England.[180] They never returned to India. Soon after they arrived in England, they were baptized at St. Mary's Church on Marylebone Road in London, as Evangelical Christians and were thereafter known by their Christian names.[181] Hollydale, the house that the children lived in, was in Bromley which was then a part of the South East County of Kent. Often called "The Garden of England", Kent with its tranquil rolling hills, stately English homes, fruit orchards and medieval castles couldn't have been more different from Hyderabad. It is usually believed that such small children forget quickly and get easily acclimatized to a change in surroundings, but

180 Heritage, Hollydale Open Space Website, U.K.

181 Interview with and research paper by Dr. Aruna Pariti on "British Residency", Department of History, Osmania Women's College (Former British Residency), Hyderabad, India. February, 2022.

there is sufficient reason to believe that the siblings did yearn terribly for their parents. After all, James and Khair had been attentive, loving parents, whose lives had completely revolved around their children. It was, of course, fortunate that the siblings were sent to England together. Back then, there were far too many examples of Anglo-Indian siblings being separated from each other solely on the basis of the colour of their skin. Often, the darker ones were made to stay back in India whereas the fairer ones who "fitted in" better were shipped off to their English families.[182] Obviously, those children then went on to lead completely different lives, never seeing each other again. Mercifully, that was not the case with Ali and Noor.

Ali and Noor, who later came to be known by their Christian names William George Kirkpatrick and Katherine Aurora (Kitty) Kirkpatrick, went on to lead very comfortable lives in England. There was no dearth of material comfort, since they were well taken care of by their grandfather as well as the inheritances their parents left them. They were both given the best of education, though William had a tougher life after a burn accident due to which his left arm had to be amputated. He did graduate from Oxford University though, got married and had children as well. Sadly, like his parents, he passed away very young, at the age of twenty-seven.

Kitty grew up to be a beautiful lady, known far and wide for her striking looks. The Scottish historian and philosopher, Thomas Carlyle, first met her in the year 1824 and was so taken with her that he made her his muse for his novel and memoirs. He thought of her as a dreamy, romantic young lady and it was in fact, one particular incident when he chanced upon her with some roses in an open

182 Garcha, Ciara. *The Curious Case of Kitty Kirkpatrick*. Our Shared Cultural Heritage. 4 August 2020.

conservatory, that inspired the character *Blumine*, the Rose-goddess of *Sartor Resartus*, Carlyle's famous literary work. He also wrote about her in his work *Reminiscences*, as, "*...her birth, as I afterward found, an Indian romance, mother a sublime begum, father a ditto English official, mutually adoring, wedding, living withdrawn in their own private paradise, Romance famous in the East.*"[183]

Carlyle and Kitty lost touch after Carlyle's marriage to Jane Welsh but crossed paths again in 1868 and renewed their friendship.

Having inherited a considerable fortune, Kitty led a luxurious life in England. She was very well acquainted with several of her paternal cousins, including Julia Strachey, the daughter of Colonel William Kirkpatrick. Kitty lived with Julia for a while and the two women enjoyed a close friendship.[184] She later went on to marry a British Army Officer and had seven children with him, four of whom survived. Two of those apparently, were mirror images of their maternal grandparents.

At a time when child-rearing in aristocratic families, both Indian and British, was left entirely to the dais and nannies, Khair-un-Nissa had been an involved, loving, devoted mother. It is sad to think that the children had to completely sever ties with their Indian family in Hyderabad and even more heart-breaking that they never saw their mother again, after that final farewell outside the Residency. The heartening bit though is that Kitty did manage to make contact with her maternal grandmother, Sharaf-un-Nissa many, many years later. Even though she had spent her entire life

183 Carlyle and "Irving's London Circle": Some Unpublished Letters by Thomas Carlyle and Mrs. Edward Strachey. Vol 69, No. 5 pp 1135-1149. J. Calder, Grace. Cambridge University Press. Dec 1954.

184 Ibid.

in England, she candidly wrote about pining for her maternal family and India.[185] That should not have been surprising to anyone. After all, India was the country of her birth and an integral part of her heritage. Ironically, the reunion was routed via Henry Russell, who eventually facilitated the reconnection between grandmother and granddaughter. Of course, Kitty spoke no Persian and Sharaf-un-Nissa did not speak English, but when did love ever need a language to be expressed? Even though the two never met physically, they exchanged a series of emotional letters in which Kitty wrote about how much she had thought of her mother throughout her life, even recalling snippets of her early years in Hyderabad, including specific details of the places where she used to spend time and play in the Residency. The final farewell seemed to have left a deep impact on her, and her last memory of her mother was of the moments when the palanquins were being carried away and Khair-un-Nissa sat on the steps of the portico, wailing and tearing at her long, beautiful hair. That was the last image of her mother that seemed to have forever imprinted itself in the three-year-old's mind. Painful though the memory must have been, Kitty it seems, did not allow herself to forget. After all, the memories were all that were left of her life in India.

Titled "The Kirkpatrick Children", the portrait which Khair had been desperately hankering after, seemed to have had its own path to travel, just like its subjects. After Chinnery borrowed it from Khair, it stayed with him for a while. Eventually, Henry Russell did manage to get it back from Chinnery, though Khair-un-Nissa was not able to see it. She had already passed away by then. It was heart-breaking

185 Garcha, Ciara. *The Curious Case of Kitty Kirkpatrick.* Our Shared Cultural Heritage. August 4th, 2020.

to think how much Khair had yearned to recover this one reminder, one memento of her children, the one prized possession that she loved most in the world, and that when it did finally make its way back to Hyderabad, it was too late for her. Anyway, it remained in Russell's possession and after his retirement, it adorned a wall in his country home in Swallowfield, Berkshire. After Russell's death in 1852 and as requested in his will, the portrait was finally handed over to its rightful owner, Kitty Kirkpatrick. It stayed in Kitty's family until 1960. After having spent 120 years in England, this portrait now hangs in a boardroom of Hong Kong and Shanghai Bank as a part of a private collection.[186] Strangers who view it must be seeing two beautiful children dressed in traditional Hyderabadi clothes and strings of pearls, the girl's arm draped around the boy's shoulders. People must be admiring it for the glorious use of colours and the fine detailing of the facial features and expressions, for after all, this was easily one of George Chinnery's most stunning masterpieces, a true work of genius that brought him incredible fame from around the world. That of course, is not all that this portrait is. This portrait is also a part of a legacy – a legacy of two people who loved each other so completely that they gave up everything to be with each other. It is a part of a legacy of two families, two empires, two separate worlds, that came together in one momentous, fateful moment when a tall, handsome British officer and a beautiful, young Mughal princess saw each other for the very first time and fell in love.

186 William and Catherine Aurora, children of Lieutenant Colonel James Achilles Kirkpatrick. Yale University Library. Digital Collections.

Glossary

Adhan – The Muslim call to prayer

Alhamdulillah – Praise be to God

Angrakhas – An outer robe with long sleeves worn by men in South Asia.

Aqiqah – The Islamic tradition of the sacrifice of an animal on the occasion of a child's birth.

Attar – A fragrant essential oil

Azizam – Sweetheart

Baghaar-e-Baingan – A Hyderabadi eggplant curry

Bajuband – Bejewelled armlet

Bazaars – Market in South Asia, the Middle East or North Africa

Beedi – A type of cigarette made of unprocessed tobacco wrapped in leaves.

Begum – A Muslim woman of high rank

Bhakti – Devotional worship directed to a supreme deity

Bibi – A respectful title for women in South Asia

Bindis – A decorative mark worn in the middle of the forehead by Indian women, especially Hindus.

Biryanis – A mixed rice dish originating from South Asia

Bismillah – A cultural ceremony which marks the start for a child in learning to recite the Qur'an in its Arabic script.

Bozorg – An old lady

Chai – Tea

Chandbalis – Moon shaped earrings

Chhota Hazri – A light meal eaten very early in the morning

Chilla – A 40-day period of confinement after childbirth

Chokar – A necklace that fits very closely round someone's neck

Churidar – Tight trousers worn by people from South Asia

Daak – Post

Dais – Wet nurses or mid-wives

Dargah – The shrine of a Muslim saint

Dastarkhwan – A big ceremonial tablecloth used across Central and South Asia.

Deorhi – A mansion or palace

Dhobi Ghat – A laundry in South and Central Asia

Divan – A long, low sofa without a back or arms

Diwan – A collection of poems by one author

Diwan – A finance minister or prime minister

Dupatta – A scarf worn in India

Durbar – The court of an Indian ruler

Eshgham – "My love" in Persian

Fakir – A religious ascetic who lives solely on alms.

Ghazals – A lyrical poem in Middle Eastern and Indian literature and music

Hadith – A collection of traditions containing sayings of Prophet Muhammad

Haleem – A stew composed of meat, lentil and pounded wheat made into a thick paste.

Hookah – An oriental tobacco pipe with a long, flexible tube which draws the smoke through water contained in a bowl.

Hookahburdars – Hookah bearer

Inshallah – God willing

Iqamah – The second call to Islamic prayer

Jagir – A feudal land grant

Jamas – A long coat popular in South Asia during the Mughal period

Jannat – Paradise

Jharokhas – A stone window projecting from the wall face of a building overlooking a street, market, court or any other open space.

Jhoomar – An ornament worn by women on the forehead

Joon – A Persian word of endearment, dear

Kabutar Khana – Pigeon house

Kalima – The formal content of the Islamic declaration of faith

Kathak – A type of Indian classical dance with alternating passages of mime and dancing

Kesar – Saffron

Khada dupatta – An upright stole which is the traditional wedding dress of Hyderabadi Muslim brides in the Indian subcontinent.

Khansama – A male cook

Khussas – A closed shoe with an extended curved toe

Kurta – A loose collarless shirt of a type worn by people in South Asia

Lori – Lullaby

Maman – Mother

Manjeera – A traditional percussion instrument from India

Mansabdar – High civil or military officials

Masha Allah – What God has willed

Maulvi – A learned Muslim who ministers to the religious needs of others

Mehfils – A gathering to entertain or praise someone

Mor ka naach – The dance of the peacock

Mulligatawny soup – A lentil soup with South Indian origin

Munshi – An Indian secretary

Mushairas – A poetic symposium, it is an event where poets gather to perform their works. A mushaira is part of the culture of north India, Pakistan and the Deccan, particularly among the Hyderabadi Muslims, and it is regarded as a forum for free self-expression.

Musnud – A cushioned seat used as a throne in India.

Nana – Maternal grandfather

Nazar – A gift of money offered to bring good fortune

Neemas – An undergarment for the upper body

Nikah – An Islamic marriage contract

Nuriya Syeds – A sect of people from Persia

Omrah – A person of high rank or eminence in a Muslim court in India.

Paan – Betelnut

Paidan – A footrest

Patang naach – The kite dance imitating both the kite and the kite flyer.

Peshkar – The chief clerk supervising the work of a department

Purdah – The practice in certain Muslim and Hindu societies of screening women from men or strangers.

Qahar ka naach – The pallbearer's dance, erotic and suggestive dance performed as the finale

Qubool hai – I accept

Razai – A cotton quilt

Sahib – A polite title or form of address for a man

Sahib Allum – Lord of the Universe

Sahib Begum – Ladyship

Sarangi – An Indian bowed musical instrument

Sari – A garment consisting of a length of cotton or silk elaborately draped around the body, traditionally worn by women from South Asia.

Satlada – A necklace that is made of 7 strings of pearls and gemstones

Sayyids – Muslims claiming descent from Muhammad

Sehra – A headdress worn by the groom during Pakistani, Indian and Bangladeshi weddings

Shahada – The Muslim profession of faith

Shamiana – A marquee

Sheesham – Indian rosewood

Sherbet- A cooling drink of sweet diluted fruit juices.

Shikampuri kebabs – A spiced kebab made from chicken or meat

Shikaris – A professional hunter or guide

Sipahsalars – Army commander

Surahi – An Indian clay pot with a long neck

Syrah – A popular red wine produced from a dark skinned grape variety.

Tabla - A pair of small hand drums used in Indian music

Tahneek – An Islamic ceremony of touching the lips of a new-born with honey or dates.

Tandoor – A clay oven used in South Asia

Thumri – A vocal genre or style of Indian music

Topis – An Indian cap

Unani – A system of medicine practised in parts of India, thought to be derived via medieval Muslim physicians.

Urs – A pilgrimage to the shrine of a Sufi saint

Vakil – An agent or representative especially of political importance in India.

Ya Allah – Oh Lord

Zardozi – Embroidery worked with gold and silver thread

Zenana – The part of the house for the seclusion of women

Interview with Mr. M.A. Qayyum, Historian and Former Deputy Director, Department of Archaeology and Museums, Hyderabad. March, 2022.

Interview with Rana Safvi. Historian and Writer. May, 2022.

Kirkpatrick, William (1754-1812). Dictionary of National Biography, 1885-1900. U.K.

Kugle, Scott. *When Sun Meets Moon – Gender, Eros and Ecstasy in Urdu Poetry (Islamic Civilization and Muslim Networks).* USA. University of North Carolina Press. 2016.

Kumar, Krishna R. When the sun set on Seringapatam. *The Hindu.* 4 May 2017.

Laslocky, Megan. *The Little Book of Heartbreak: Love gone wrong through the ages.* USA. Plume, a member of Penguin Group, USA. January, 2013.

Malcolm, John. Private Secretary – Scandal in Hyderabad. Malcolm – Soldier, Diplomat, Ideologue of British India: The Life of Sir John Malcolm. UK. John Donald – An Imprint of Birlinn Ltd. 2014.

Mani, Fiona. *Guns and Shikaris: The rise of the sahib's hunting ethos and the fall of the subaltern poacher in British India, 1750-1947.* Research Repository, West Virginia University, 2012.

Marshall, P.J. *Eighteenth Century India.* Oxford Dictionary of National Biography. May, 2005.

Meaden, David. *Hidden Letters: When Documents Contain a Surprise.* Untold Lives Blog, British Library, India Office Records.

Meehan, Sumayyah. Welcome a New Born to the Way of Faith. *Khaleej Times.* 16 May 2008.

Mukhoty, Ira. *Akbar - The Great Mughal.* India. Aleph Book Company. April, 2020.

Naidu, T. Appala. Masula Heritage Sites. *The Hindu.* 3 June 2007.

Nanisetti, Sarish. Mir Alam Bahadur is remembered for his gifts to Hyderabad. *The Hindu.* 30 March, 2019.

Original Will of Lieutenant Colonel James Achilles Kirkpatrick. The National Archives. United Kingdom.
Scan here to read the full will.

Pandharipande, Reeti and Nadimpally, Lasya. A Brief History of the Nizams of Hyderabad. *Outlook Traveller.* 5 August 2017.

Prakash, Dr. Satya *An Outline of Ancestral History of Salar Jungs.* Hyderabad: Published by The Salar Jung Museum.

R. Farr, James. *Who was William Hickey? A Crafted Life in Georgian England and Imperial India.* U.S.A. Routledge. 26 Sep 2019.

Ramanathan, Aditya. Battle of Assaye. *The Wire.* September, 2016.

Saini, Anu. *Physicians of Colonial India.* National Library of Medicine, India. July – Sept, 2016.

Self Portrait. George Chinnery. The Collection. European Paintings. The MET, New York. 1825-28.

Stewart, Courtney, A. *Feminine Power of the Deccan.* The Metropolitan Museum of Art, New York. Dept of Islamic Art.

Stewart, Stanley. India's Sleeping Beauty Awakes. *The Times,* UK. 28 November 2010.

Swami, V. Narayan. *A Many-tinted, Radiant Aurora: George Chinnery's Kitty Kirkpatrick.* Books Society of India. 24 July 2014.

Thathipalli, Mallik. The moon-cheeked poet and her forgotten legacy. *The Hindu. Business Line.* March 29th, 2021.

The Hyderabad Political System and its Participants. Karen Leonard. *The Journal of Asian Studies* Vol. 30, No. 3 (May, 1971), pp. 569-582. The Association for Asian Studies

The Residency. Online Gallery. British Library.

The Russells of Swallowfield Park. Swallowfield Park Case Study, UK. East India Company at Home, 1757-1857.

University of Chicago Library, Guide to the J. Kirkpatrick Collection 1810-1811.

Wilkinson, Callie. *Relationships between the Political Residents of the English East India Company and their munshis, 1798-1818.* Wolfson College, University of Cambridge.

Women in Deccani Painting. Select artworks from the collection of Salar Jung Museum, Hyderabad, India. Google Arts and Culture.